DEAR TO ME

DEAR TO ME

100 New Zealanders Write About Their Favourite Poems

AMNESTY INTERNATIONAL
www.amnesty.org.nz

RANDOM HOUSE
NEW ZEALAND

A catalogue record for this book is available from the National Library
of New Zealand

A RANDOM HOUSE BOOK
published by
Random House New Zealand
18 Poland Road, Glenfield, Auckland, New Zealand
www.randomhouse.co.nz

Random House International
Random House
20 Vauxhall Bridge Road
London, SW1V 2SA
United Kingdom

Random House Australia (Pty) Ltd
20 Alfred Street, Milsons Point, Sydney,
New South Wales 2061, Australia

Random House South Africa Pty Ltd
Isle of Houghton
Corner Boundary Road and Carse O'Gowrie
Houghton 2198, South Africa

Random House Publishers India Private Ltd
301 World Trade Tower, Hotel Intercontinental Grand Complex,
Barakhamba Lane, New Delhi 110 001, India

First published 2007

ISBN 978 1 86941 832 8

Text design: Jacinda Torrance, Verso Visual
Cover design: Alan Deare, Inhouse Design
Printed in China by Everbest Printing Co Ltd

Contents

Foreword

When Amnesty International first conceived of this poetry book, one of the most exciting aspects was the opportunity to engage the talent and enthusiasm of one of our school groups. This project promised to not only raise the profile of Amnesty's human rights work, but also to encourage the pupils to believe in the power to influence their world. The idea was for the students and their teacher to write to 100 well-known New Zealanders and ask them, 'What is your favourite poem and please tell us why.'

Auckland Girls' Grammar School has a proud tradition of empowering young women and this is reflected in the enthusiasm and support extended to this project.

The list of acknowledgements is long but special mention must be made of the principal Liz Thomson, whose encouragement of the book from inception allowed it to progress quickly, and Libby Giles, social sciences teacher, with whom it has been a pleasure to work. Her energy and unwavering enthusiasm are an inspiration to all.

Libby's leadership and commitment to the Amnesty School Group allowed the lovely young women in the group – Vaitaua Mauala, Cleopatra Matthews, Esther Keown, Geraldine Worner, Lisa Zhang and Shika Narayan – to participate in an exciting and meaningful project through which they express their commitment to human rights. The journey they have begun through their involvement in the book will, I hope, continue and allow them to nurture a belief in their real power to influence and bring about change.

Thanks must also be given to Nicola Legat and Catherine O'Loughlin of Random House for their vision and belief in the idea and to Tony Lindsay of Amnesty for contributing the concept. We are honoured to have Bill Manhire as patron. His insightful and sensitive involvement is portrayed beautifully in his introduction. And of course, to the poets whose work has inspired these wonderful responses and to everyone who has taken the time to contribute such thoughtful explanations we give our warmest thanks and appreciation.

Amnesty International Aotearoa thanks all who have been involved in bringing this book to life.

LINDA WORNER
Relationship Manager
Amnesty International Aotearoa

Beyond Mint Sauce: an Introduction

In 1981 the New Zealand Prime Minister Robert Muldoon gave an address to the Worshipful Company of Butchers in London. Here is a little of what he said:

> There's a story told about Sir Walter Scott, who was walking with his wife at Abbotsford one day when they came upon a flock of sheep with new-born lambs playing about them. 'It's no wonder,' he said to his wife, 'that poets from the earliest ages have made the lamb the emblem of peace and innocence.' 'They are indeed, delightful animals,' replied Lady Scott, 'especially with mint sauce.'
>
> Poetry is all very well, but we in New Zealand are most interested in the mint sauce end of the animal.

The prime ministerial words were actually written by a witty member of the Ministry of Foreign Affairs, but probably Sir Robert enjoyed reading them aloud, and surely the butchers – for some reason I imagine them all sitting in freshly pressed, striped aprons – would have chuckled.

There is something about New Zealanders that values the pragmatic. 'What is it for?' is the first question we ask of something. Or, 'What does he/she/it *do*?' The problem with poetry is that we are never quite sure what it can do. There it is, and we meet it at school, and sometimes a poem or two sticks – but it doesn't seem to help with the balance of payments. Poetry has no value in the marketplace. You could sell a banana on Queen Street far more quickly than a poem.

And yet . . . every time we go to a naming ceremony, a wedding, a funeral, a memorial event like Anzac Day, there are the poems among us, at the very centre of our lives. Worth nothing, they are somehow worth everything – particularly during those rites of passage when we are drawn together by what we have in common.

This book has been brought together on behalf of Amnesty International, which works for all those things we have – or ought to have – in common. These include freedom from discrimination and, especially, freedom of conscience and expression. Imaginative literature, and poetry in particular, have always been at the heart of these freedoms. We can safely assume that all of the public figures who have generously shared a favourite poem endorse them, too.

What kind of poems have they chosen? An astonishing range, is the answer. I find it enormously encouraging that so many of these poems are by New Zealand writers. (That wouldn't have been the case 50 years ago.) I find it encouraging, too, that so many poems have been chosen for the wonderful things they do with words as much as for the things they say. The great Russian poet, Osip Mandelstam (1891–1938), was put to death in Stalinist Russia because his poems chose beauty and lyricism over obedience to the state. 'Only in Russia,' he once wrote, 'is poetry respected – it gets people killed. Is there anywhere else where poetry is so common a motive for murder?'

It's not my role to analyse the poetry selections here beyond acknowledging the ways they connect with the humanity of those who chose them. Perhaps, however, I can note that many of the poems in *Dear to Me* – and many New Zealanders by extension – have that most dangerous thing of all, a lively sense of humour. If the poems we once met in the schoolroom intimidated us with their high, impenetrable seriousness, that is no longer the case – or not, at least, in the lives we have all gone on to lead. Most of us know that poetry can entertain and give pleasure, even as it makes us think or reflect.

Three poems have been chosen twice. One is R.A.K. Mason's 'On the Swag', a pragmatic declension of the Christian story, very much fitted to some sort of New Zealand reality. (The contexts change, of course. Swagmen no longer wander the countryside, knocking on farmhouse doors; these days they live in the middle of our towns and cities.)

Another twice-chosen poem is Coleridge's 'Kubla Khan', a poem written in 1798, very nearly abandoned by its author as an incomprehensible fragment, and now acknowledged as one of the great poems in the English language. Which brings us again to the world of prime ministers. My guess is that Helen Clark and Sir Geoffrey Palmer have chosen Coleridge's poem partly for the astonishing way in which it mixes music and mystery. And yet it is in some ways a very straightforward poem. Within its incantations, it tells a little story about something most politicians understand: the limits of earthly power. Kubla Khan's wondrous pleasure-dome, an assertion of material dominion, turns out to be nothing compared to the greater powers of the natural world, which declare themselves when the underground river erupts into his fiefdom. Kubla has raised his towers in earthquake country.

Yet the thing which excites the poet is neither Kubla Khan's dome nor the power of a subterranean river. Rather it is the marriage of the two realms, the secular and worldly with the sacred and the natural. The result, revealed in the miracle of the 'sunny pleasure-dome with caves of ice', is what only an artist can make – a daring yet harmonious paradox that makes us gasp with awe. In the end, 'Kubla Khan' is about the greatness of poetic power.

Amnesty International is interested in power, too. What are its proper and productive uses? How can we resist those who wish to use their power against us? Why does power so often grow from the barrel of a gun? The writers of these poems, and the men and women who chose them, along with the students at Auckland Girls' Grammar who worked so hard to bring this book into being, all have good hearts. It is good to hear their voices among the many who seek answers to such questions.

BILL MANHIRE

Dear to Me Patron, poet, Director of the International Institute of Modern Letters, Victoria University of Wellington

Michele A'Court

COMEDIAN, WRITER, SOCIAL COMMENTATOR

Dear Shika,

I must have read this poem shortly after it was first published in 1982 – though I don't remember ever *not* knowing it. I would have been 21 then, and living in a student flat in Christchurch.

I read it then as a protest poem: a protest against the grinding drudgery of women's lives. I loved its conversational tone – an ordinary voice talking about the ordinary things that drive us mad. And I loved the list that had the pleasant and the inane sitting side by side – 'I cleaned the bathroom like mad and picked some flowers and wrote some letters and some cheques . . .' And I loved its rhythm, its accelerating pace as it spirals upwards – and the exhilaration you feel as you discover it spirals *upwards*, rather than descends.

For 25 years, it has continued to play in my head as I do the housework. It's impossible for me to scrub out the shower without thinking of a cat's big green eyes ticking away, and I laugh out loud if I look up at the clock as I vacuum and it says Ten to five. But it's less of a protest poem for me now, more of a celebration – that despite the fact that so much of our lives is inevitably taken up with the tedious and crushingly ordinary, inside our heads we can still fly.

Michele A'Court

Timepiece

I got home from work and looked at
my watch and it said
Ten to five, so I did the washing and
picked some greens and tidied up the
kitchen and sat down and had a cup of coffee,
and looked at my watch and still it said
Ten to five, so I did some ironing and
made the beds and thought Hell I might
get all the housework done in one day
for a change, then looked at my watch
but nope, no change, and I turned on the
radio and it said Ten to five, so
I cleaned the bathroom like mad and
picked some flowers and wrote some
letters and some cheques and scrubbed
the kitchen floor and got started on the
windows – by this time I was getting a bit
desperate I can tell you, I was thinking
alternately Yay! soon there'll be no more to
do and I'll be free, and Jeez what if I
RUN OUT? I did in fact run out, and out,
and out, past the church clock saying
Ten to five and the cat on the corner with
big green eyes ticking away, and up into the
sky past the telephone wires, and
up into the blue, watchless, matchless, timeless
cloud-curtains, where I hide, and
it is silent, silent.

CILLA MCQUEEN

Dr Rod Alley

SEMI-RETIRED POLITICAL SCIENTIST, INTERNATIONAL RELATIONS
COMMENTATOR, ENTHUSIAST FOR NUCLEAR DISARMAMENT

Dear Lisa,

Like many other contributors I have a James K. Baxter
favourite, or several in fact. When she was a teaching student,
my elder sister Judith would have long conversations with
Baxter in a well-known local Wellington eatery called The
Green Parrot (it survives today), and I remember her bringing
home the first typed copies of Baxter's poems for children.
Baxter would from time to time drop in on my father, a
librarian, to borrow ten shillings to see him though the week.

My first choice, then, is Baxter's 'Lament for Barney Flanagan',
followed closely by his 'Election 1960'.

Rod Alley

Lament for Barney Flanagan
Licensee of the Hesperus Hotel

Flanagan got up on a Saturday morning,
Pulled on his pants while the coffee was warming;
He didn't remember the doctor's warning,
    'Your heart's too big, Mr Flanagan.'

Barney Flanagan, sprung like a frog
From a wet root in an Irish bog –
May his soul escape from the tooth of the dog!
    God have mercy on Flanagan.

Barney Flanagan R.I.P.
Rode to his grave on Hennessy's
Like a bottle-cork boat in the Irish Sea.
    The bell-boy rings for Flanagan.

Barney Flanagan, ripe for a coffin,
Eighteen stone and brandy-rotten,
Patted the housemaid's velvet bottom —
    'Oh, is it you, Mr Flanagan?'

The sky was bright as a new milk token.
Bill the Bookie and Shellshock Hogan
Waited outside for the pub to open —
    'Good day, Mr Flanagan.'

At noon he was drinking in the lounge bar corner
With a sergeant of police and a racehorse owner
When the Angel of Death looked over his shoulder —
    'Could you spare a moment, Flanagan?'

Oh the deck was cut; the bets were laid;
But the very last card that Barney played
Was the Deadman's Trump, the bullet of Spades —
    'Would you like more air, Mr Flanagan?'

The priest came running but the priest came late
For Barney was banging at the Pearly Gate.
St Peter said, 'Quiet! You'll have to wait
    For a hundred masses, Flanagan.'

The regular boys and the loud accountants
Left their nips and their seven-ounces
As chickens fly when the buzzard pounces —
    'Have you heard about old Flanagan?'

Cold in the parlour Flanagan lay
Like a bride at the end of her marriage day.
The Waterside Workers' Band will play
    A brass goodbye to Flanagan.

While publicans drink to their profits still
While lawyers flock to be in at the kill,
While Aussie barmen milk the till
    We will remember Flanagan.

For Barney had a send-off and no mistake.
He died like a man for his country's sake;
And the Governor-General came to his wake.
    Drink again to Flanagan!

Despise not, O Lord, the work of Thine own hands
And let light perpetual shine upon him.

JAMES K. BAXTER

Murray Ball

CARTOONIST

Dear Cleo,

I wrote the following poem for my introduction to *Footrot Flats* 7, concerning the death of the cat, Horse. It was not Shakespeare but meant a lot to me.

Most Footrot Flats characters are imaginary. They inhabit a place just over the horizon of my mind. I visit them and become involved with the Dog, Wal, Cooch and the rest. But Horse was real.

He stalked into my life through the rhubarb patch, ignored the yard broom I threw at him and beat up our two tame toms. In vain did I drive him away. He would retire into a blackberry bush and watch me caper and hurl abuse and gumboots at him. When I had run out of breath and boots he would saunter out and rub against my leg.

He was a concrete block of a cat – with muscles hard as green quinces.

He fought a lot – so he often had abscesses. He would limp for a while and a bit later a raw crater the size of an egg cup would appear on his side. A similar wound would lay our cats up for a fortnight. Horse simply curled up on the lawn and let the rain fall on him. Perhaps it cooled his temperature.

A time came when we introduced two female kittens to the household. We watched their first encounter with Horse with some apprehension. He did not tear them to pieces. Within a week they were sucking his toe pads and stealing his eels. However should a wandering tom appear there would be screams in the night, a pile of foreign fur under the camellia in the morning and perhaps a week or two later another abscess would appear on Horse's body.

A collie dog, fresh off its chain, bright-eyed and eager, snuffled up our drive. He ran nose to nose into Horse. I felt for his innocence. He gave a playful woof. Horse advanced a pace. The dog's ears drooped slightly and he withdrew his face. Woof, woof? The hair on Horse's back rose. He seemed to double his size. His stubby tail bristled like a lavatory brush. He moved forward stiff legged, lime eyed and humourless. The dog did one or two limp bounds, yipped uncertainly and reversed back down into the road. With a final, face-saving whiffle he turned and trotted on down the road, obviously with more important things to attend to. Horse held the gate.

Now Horse is dead.

Rats rejoice, strays wander in and out at will. Wekas steal our ducklings and there is a huge vacuum on the hills where a scarred black and white cat used to push through the yellow grass-heads.

Now he lives only over the horizon of my mind, tormenting the Dog and haunting the hills and swamps of Footrot Flats.

Thanks, Horse.

Murray Ball

Horse is Dead

Horse is dead.
He disdained Death
Until it pulled him to the ground
And gnawed his entrails out.
Your bared teeth
And twitching claws
Were of no use, were they old Horse?
Even you could not stare down Death.
Horse would not die.
Death wrenched, kicked, barked its knuckles
And swore.
And the old bag of nuts and bolts and steel pipes
Rattled and clanked
But would not be still.

I couldn't stand it.
I hit Horse between the eyes with a hammer.
He died in silence.
It tore my heart.

He looked as though he slept
As he had done all those years on the lawn.
The rain falling
And lying like small glass balls
On his black and white fur.

I buried him under a young pohutukawa on the hill.
Ironwood, the pohutukawa
And Horse —

Horse is dead.
Long live Horse.

Arthur Baysting

WRITER

Dear Libby,

When I was young I wanted to be a poet and I got Janet Frame's book of poems, *The Pocket Mirror*, out of the library. 'Dunedin Poem' was the first in the book and it changed mysteriously each time I read it. The opening verse reminded me of Shakespeare and, when she asked questions about the gloomy weather, it reminded me of a lost Bob Dylan song.

Then she threw down an image so violent that it took my breath away.

'The tramlines are torn from their sockets.'

It stayed in my mind, and comes back every time I see machinery tearing things up in the city. I didn't know then that, when Janet was younger, she had long periods of electric shock treatment in a mental hospital. If you've read her own story (or seen the film, *An Angel at My Table*), you may suspect the line is not just about Dunedin's transport system.

The last brilliant pictures change again: to flowering trees and Janet going down to the beach, nearly 20 years later, to do what all New Zealanders do – to stare at the ocean waves.

I did write poetry for a while and then turned into a songwriter. And these days I still wish I could write like Janet Frame.

Arthur

Dunedin Poem

Here I've gone down with the sun
written syllables till time has surprised me
with the fact of his consistency.
I love not you but the sun's going down
so easily.

Soon will the days be dark? Will the mists come,
the rain blow from Signal Hill down Northeast Valley
that in winter lies in shadow?
I never remember the sun, in Northeast Valley.

The tramlines are torn from their sockets.
Things do not suffer as we supposed.
People suffer more than we supposed.
The buses tread softly, jerk to a stop, the doors slide open.
I climb in, travelling to where
down a long street lined with flowering cherry trees I walked
nineteen years ago
to stare at the waves on St. Clair beach.

JANET FRAME

Gavin Bishop

CHILDREN'S AUTHOR AND ILLUSTRATOR

Dear Va,

This is the classic schoolboy's poem. I loved it from the first moment I heard it – probably in the fifth form (year 11). In fact my whole class loved it, even though we had to learn it by heart. We used to chant it aloud. Its rollicking rhythm and predictable rhyme totally satisfied our 15-year-old expectations of a poem. The tight structure left no dangling threads. The last verse wrapped it up as neatly as an egg.

As far as we were concerned, nothing much happened, action wise, after the first two verses, but the later scenes conjured up an atmosphere as heroic as anything we might have seen in an Errol Flynn flick at a Saturday matinee.

I still enjoy this poem now as much as I did then. It only occurred to me recently though, that we were never told at school who Sennacherib was or why an avenging angel struck down the Assyrian army. And I can't remember anyone asking about it. We must have been satisfied with the way the poem was. The patterns of the language and its rich imagery were enough.

Gavin Bishop

The Destruction of Sennacherib

The Assyrian came down like the wolf on the fold,
And his cohorts were gleaming in purple and gold;
And the sheen of their spears was like stars on the sea,
When the blue wave rolls nightly on deep Galilee.

Like the leaves of the forest when Summer is green,
That host with their banners at sunset were seen:
Like the leaves of the forest when Autumn hath blown,
That host on the morrow lay withered and strown.

For the Angel of Death spread his wings on the blast,
And breathed in the face of the foe as he passed;
And the eyes of the sleepers waxed deadly and chill,
And their hearts but once heaved, and for ever grew still!

And there lay the steed with his nostril all wide,
But through it there rolled not the breath of his pride;
And the foam of his gasping lay white on the turf,
And cold as the spray of the rock-beating surf.

And there lay the rider distorted and pale,
With the dew on his brow, and the rust on his mail:
And the tents were all silent, the banners alone,
The lances unlifted, the trumpet unblown.

And the widows of Ashur are loud in their wail,
And the idols are broke in the temple of Baal;
And the might of the Gentile, unsmote by the sword,
Hath melted like snow in the glance of the Lord!

GEORGE GORDON, LORD BYRON

Don Brash

GOVERNOR OF THE RESERVE BANK 1988–2002,
LEADER OF THE NATIONAL PARTY 2003–2006

Dear Esther,

You asked me to supply a favourite poem. Alas, I have not
spent nearly as much time reading poetry in recent years as
would have been good for me, so I am sending you instead a
poem which meant a very great deal to me as a teenager in
Christchurch.

At the time, I was particularly concerned about international
conflict, and had just registered as a conscientious objector. The
poem which had such an impact was by Siegfried Sassoon, and
entitled 'The Rear-Guard'. It was written in 1917, during the
First World War.

With best wishes.

Yours sincerely,

Don Brash

The Rear-Guard

(Hindenburg Line, April 1917)

Groping along the tunnel, step by step,
He winked his prying torch with patching glare
From side to side, and sniffed the unwholesome air.

Tins, boxes, bottles, shapes too vague to know;
A mirror smashed, the mattress from a bed;
And he, exploring fifty feet below
The rosy gloom of battle overhead.

Tripping, he grabbed the wall; saw some one lie
Humped at his feet, half-hidden by a rug,
And stooped to give the sleeper's arm a tug.
'I'm looking for headquarters.' No reply.
'God blast your neck!' (For days he'd had no sleep)
'Get up and guide me through this stinking place.'
Savage, he kicked a soft, unanswering heap,
And flashed his beam across the livid face
Terribly glaring up, whose eyes yet wore
Agony dying hard ten days before;
And fists of fingers clutched a blackening wound.

Alone he staggered on until he found
Dawn's ghost that filtered down a shafted stair
To the dazed, muttering creatures underground
Who hear the boom of shells in muffled sound.
At last, with sweat of horror in his hair,
He climbed through darkness to the twilight air,
Unloading hell behind him step by step.

SIEGFRIED SASSOON

Steve Braunias

JOURNALIST

Dear Lisa,

Sorry not to have replied earlier – very bad manners not to do so. As follows is one of many New Zealand poems I really like. It's by Kevin Ireland, first published in *Islands*, March 1980, and it's about a bronze bust a sculptor called Anthony Stones made of Ireland.

Stones as Sculptor

This is a fine piece of work
the sculpture you are making today

it has my eyes and nose and moustache
like a kit bought in a joke shop

but how should we be serious about it?
when I am transmuted from clay to bronze

my children will only want to knock me
and make me go BONG

KEVIN IRELAND

Best, and thanks for asking me to contribute,

Steve

Bernard Brown

LAW LECTURER, POET

Dear Cleo,

Thank you for your invitation to contribute to *Dear to Me*.
Yes, I accept.

My choice will be a poem by D.J. Enright, 'The Terrible Shears'
— which I'll have to hunt up. Dennis Enright was a friend and
colleague in Singapore in the early years of Lee Kuan Yew's
rigid 'detention without trial' regime (which still obtains) and
Dennis was arrested while delivering his inaugural lecture from
the Chair of English.

Dennis Enright was the most unassuming yet magnetic person
I have met. Of humble English Midlands origin, by his poetry
and his critical writings he found his way into professorships
at (then) exotic locations such as Alexandria, Tokyo and
Bangkok.

Looking back to 1960, it was predictable that Dennis would
turn up at Singapore University, where in his lanky, laconic
way he ignited student and staff interest to a point at which
the security police felt it necessary to arrest him during his
inaugural lecture from the Chair of English. Being Dennis, he
brushed aside the violation and stayed another dozen years to
quietly 'cock a snook' at Authority's pretentions, to jolly up
pupils, and engage with intriguing folk such as ex-detainees
(without trial), the doctor–author Han Suyin (*Love is a Many
Splendoured Thing*), beachcombers and young writers. And he
polished my poor poetry.

Dennis knew my favourite book of his was *The Terrible Shears*
(about his hard childhood) but, in Singapore days, we idly

shared a smile when a Dr Benjamin Sheares, who had
passionately pioneered vasectomies in that city, was appointed
Head of State.

The poem below (line 24), gave Dennis's book its title. It flits —
as kids do — between envy, luck, mystery and terror, and it
tweaks the ultimate object of their, and our, curiosity.

Good wishes,

Bernard Brown

Uncertainties

Our folk didn't have much
In the way of lore.

But I remember a story,
A warning against envy
And also against good fortune,
Too much for our small heads —

About a lucky man called Jim
(My uncle in Dublin I used to think,
But he was Sunny Jim)
And his friend who envied him.
Jim had the luck
He married the girl they both of them loved
And his friend envied him.
Then Jim died, and the friend
Married his widow. And then
The friend envied lucky Jim,
Asleep in peace in the churchyard.

When Granpa wasn't pushing old ladies
Through the streets of the Spa
He would cut the grass on selected graves.
Sometimes we went with him. Dogs
Had done their business on the hummocks.
The water smelt bad in the rusty vases.
The terrible shears went clack clack.

It was too much for our small heads.
Who was it that we mustn't envy —
The living or the dead?

D.J. ENRIGHT

Jaquie Brown

REPORTER, *CAMPBELL LIVE*

Dear Libby and Shika,

I love this poem.

I love it because it brings a softness to the inevitable.

Richard Langston has an amazing ability to capture life and feeling and not make it floral or limp.

He writes with humour and it really appeals to me.

Jaquie Brown

Sleeping Arrangements

I beside you and you beside me
when we roll together we are heat combined
what a lovely efficiency

When we do not lie together we are apart
but we are held by ropes and tendrils
so all heat is not lost

Yet one coming day we must lie apart
confined to our narrow beds of grief.
You lie beside me and I lie beside you

And we cradle our tender bones.

RICHARD LANGSTON

Rick Bryant

MUSICIAN

Hi Libby,

When I first read 'A Takapuna Businessman Considers his Son's Death in Korea', I recognised the authority of a great voice that tells some hard stories, but also a good heart and understanding. At least, that's what I think.

Good luck with your project.

Rick Bryant

A Takapuna Businessman Considers his Son's Death in Korea

Your sailboat yawns for you in the spidery shed
Among the mangrove trunks; I watched you build it
Before they hid you under stones in a pit
In North Korean ice. Your mother's head,

High cheekbones, hard black eyes! At Cherry Farm
She waits for God, a tube-fed schizophrene
With the unwrinkled forehead of eighteen.
The harbour's death-mask sweats in summer calm.

In my wall safe I keep the fir tree cone
You gave me once. You liked your whisky-mad
Iron-gutted killjoy of a Dad;
Too well perhaps. Why did I let you groan

That rugged year, when you reached out to me
For help, down South? I thought, 'The lion's whelp
Must learn to fight the jackals without help' —
And you became a prefect. Sodomy

Is what they teach. I heard that little slut,
Your stepmother, after she'd piled me drunk
Under a blanket in my dogbox bunk,
Creep out to you in the garden hut;

I never whispered of it. Muskets blazed
From the hunched snipers of pohutukawa
The day you stole my wallet and my car
And drove to Puhoi. Now I fumble dazed

Outside the door. O Absalom, the beast
Of anger, time and age will grind my skull
To powder! Spiders web your sailboat's hull.
The sword of Joab rages in the East.

JAMES K. BAXTER

Dean Buchanan

ARTIST

Dear Esther,

When I read your letter asking for a favourite poem I immediately thought of Rimbaud and the poem 'The Cupboard'.

My friend Lud introduced me to Rimbaud in about 1972. Lud died a few years ago, way before he should have, so this poem holds a lot of memories for me.

It's a simple poem but contains a complete world.

Cheers,

Dean Buchanan

The Cupboard

It is a wide carved cupboard; the dark oak,
Very old, has taken on the pleasant quality of old people;
The cupboard is open, and gives off in its shadow
Delightful odours like a draught of old wine;

Crammed full, it is a jumble of strange old things,
Of sweet-smelling yellow linen, bits of clothing
Of women or children, of faded laces,
Of grandmother kerchiefs embroidered with griffins;

— There you would find medallions, locks
Of white or blond hair, portraits, dried flowers
Whose smell mingles with the smell of fruit.

— O cupboard of old times, you know many stories,
And you would like to tell your stories, and you murmur
When your big black doors slowly open.

ARTHUR RIMBAUD

Peter G. Bush

PHOTOGRAPHER

Dear Libby,

This evocative poem of only 15 lines and 87 words has been
an old favourite of mine, especially these lines from the last
stanza:

> Dirty British coaster with a salt-caked smoke stack
> Butting through the Channel in the mad March days

It reminds me so strongly of my own days spent at sea and
fits the description of an English freighter that I was a crewman
on back in the '50s. Not only did our ship sport a salt-caked
smoke-stack but it was also a grimy old tub, well past its
use-by date.

And who has not dreamed of watching a 'Stately Spanish
galleon coming from the Isthmus'? Masefield has managed to
capture the eternal romance of the sea — something that never
quite leaves those who have gone down to the sea in ships.

Peter G. Bush

Cargoes

Quinquireme of Nineveh from distant Ophir,
Rowing home to haven in sunny Palestine,
With a cargo of ivory,
And apes and peacocks,
Sandalwood, cedarwood, and sweet white wine.

Stately Spanish galleon coming from the Isthmus,
Dipping through the Tropics by the palm-green shores,
With a cargo of diamonds,
Emeralds, amethysts,
Topazes, and cinnamon, and gold moidores.

Dirty British coaster with a salt-caked smoke stack,
Butting through the Channel in the mad March days,
With a cargo of Tyne coal,
Road-rails, pig-lead,
Firewood, iron-ware, and cheap tin trays.

JOHN MASEFIELD

Dorothy Butler

AUTHOR, CHILDREN'S LITERATURE ADVOCATE

Dear Va,

I first met this poem more than 60 years ago, when I was a student at Auckland University. Professor Arthur Sewell, an Englishman with a fine, deep voice, read it aloud more than once; it was obviously a favourite of his.

At Auckland Girls' Grammar School I had learned to love poetry, but it was always English poetry. Now, we were introduced to the work of New Zealand poets, whose existence we had probably not suspected.

I like the earthiness of 'On the Swag', with the sudden change of tone in the last two verses. I was moved all those years ago by the spirit that pervades them: that of kindness to 'the least of these' which is a tenet of most faiths, and of humanism.

I have never lost my feeling for 'On the Swag'. I can still hear Prof. Sewell reading it.

Dorothy Butler

Sir Douglas Graham

FORMER MINISTER OF JUSTICE

Dear Ms Giles,

I have always enjoyed this short poem because it reinforces, and indeed won't let us forget, that one of the most fundamental duties we all have is to put out a helping hand to those in need.

Good luck with your project.

Kind regards,

Rt Hon Sir Douglas Graham

On the Swag

His body doubled
   under the pack
   that sprawls untidily
   on his old back
   the cold wet dead-beat
   plods up the track.

The cook peers out:
   'oh curse that old lag —
   here again
   with his clumsy swag
   made of a dirty old
   turnip bag.'

'Bring him in cook
   from the grey level sleet
   put silk on his body
   slippers on his feet,
   give him fire
   and bread and meat.

'Let the fruit be plucked
   and the cake be iced,
   the bed be snug
   and the wine be spiced
   in the old cove's night-cap:
   for this is Christ.'

R.A.K. MASON

John Campbell

HOST, *CAMPBELL LIVE*

Dear Geraldine,

Robert Lowell was born in Boston in 1917, the son of one of that aristocratic city's great patrician families: 'And this is good old Boston, The home of the bean and the cod, Where the Lowells talk to the Cabots, And the Cabots talk only to God.'

Lowell wrote brilliantly of his family. 'My Last Afternoon with Uncle Devereux Winslow' is an unflinchingly straight autobiographical poem. And he wrote brilliantly too of his family's geographical place, most famously in 'The Quaker Graveyard in Nantucket'.

But all his abilities, all his brutal insight, his passionate intelligence, his growing sense of anger at the twentieth century's 'savage servility', are never better combined than in 'For the Union Dead'.

Robert Gould Shaw was a distant relative of Robert Lowell's. He was also the white officer who led the all-Black 54th Regiment in the American Civil War. When he was shot by the soldiers of the South they buried him with his 'niggers' intending it as an insult, but his liberal, abolitionist family were proud that he lay with them in a mass grave and turned down a suggestion after the war that he be moved.

So Lowell takes Shaw's death, and a monument to Shaw and his soldiers that stands in downtown Boston, and he compares their nobility, their bravery, their heroic goodness, with Boston and America as he found them in 1960.

He searches for a monument to modern nobility, but finds only:

a commercial photograph
shows Hiroshima boiling
over a Mosler Safe, the 'Rock of Ages'
that survived the blast.

Lowell was a conscientious objector. That Mosler should use the nuclear blast in Hiroshima to sell their safe was grotesque to him.

Note too how throughout the poem his childhood stands for something lost. This culminates in a four-word sentence: 'The Aquarium is gone.' No other poet would dare to do so much with such a rudely bald phrase.

Which leaves us fallen and debased, diminished beside Colonel Shaw and his men. Everywhere ugliness asserts itself.

And so at the beginning of the '60s, a middle-aged man from one of Boston's most privileged families had begun the whistle-blowing that would later find a popular expression in the hippy movement and the music of Bob Dylan.

It is a stunningly vituperative poem. As relevant now as then. And utterly at home in a collection to raise money for Amnesty International.

John Campbell

For the Union Dead

'Relinquunt Omnia Servare Rem Publicam.'

The old South Boston Aquarium stands
in a Sahara of snow now. Its broken windows are boarded.
The bronze weathervane cod has lost half its scales.
The airy tanks are dry.

Once my nose crawled like a snail on the glass;
my hand tingled
to burst the bubbles
drifting from the noses of the cowed, compliant fish.

My hand draws back. I often sigh still
for the dark downward and vegetating kingdom
of the fish and reptile. One morning last March,
I pressed against the new barbed and galvanized

fence on the Boston Common. Behind their cage,
yellow dinosaur steamshovels were grunting
as they cropped up tons of mush and grass
to gouge their underworld garage.

Parking spaces luxuriate like civic
sandpiles in the heart of Boston.
A girdle of orange, Puritan-pumpkin colored girders
braces the tingling Statehouse,

shaking over the excavations, as it faces Colonel Shaw
and his bell-cheeked Negro infantry
on St. Gaudens' shaking Civil War relief,
propped by a plank splint against the garage's earthquake.

Two months after marching through Boston,
half the regiment was dead;
at the dedication,
William James could almost hear the bronze Negroes breathe.

Their monument sticks like a fishbone
in the city's throat.
Its Colonel is as lean
as a compass-needle.

He has an angry wrenlike vigilance,
a greyhound's gentle tautness;
he seems to wince at pleasure,
and suffocate for privacy.

He is out of bounds now. He rejoices in man's lovely,
peculiar power to choose life and die –
when he leads his black soldiers to death,
he cannot bend his back.

On a thousand small town New England greens,
the old white churches hold their air
of sparse, sincere rebellion; frayed flags
quilt the graveyards of the Grand Army of the Republic.

The stone statues of the abstract Union Soldier
grow slimmer and younger each year –
wasp-waisted, they doze over muskets
and muse through their sideburns . . .

Shaw's father wanted no monument
except the ditch,
where his son's body was thrown
and lost with his 'niggers'.

The ditch is nearer.
There are no statues for the last war here;
on Boylston Street, a commercial photograph
shows Hiroshima boiling

over a Mosler Safe, the 'Rock of Ages'
that survived the blast. Space is nearer.
When I crouch to my television set,
the drained faces of Negro school-children rise like balloons.

Colonel Shaw
is riding on his bubble,
he waits
for the blessèd break.

The Aquarium is gone. Everywhere,
giant finned cars nose forward like fish;
a savage servility
slides by on grease.

ROBERT LOWELL

Dame Silvia Cartwright

GOVERNOR-GENERAL OF NEW ZEALAND 2001–2006

Dear Lisa,

Thank you for your invitation to include my favourite poem in your publication *Dear to Me*.

My favourite poem relates to a much earlier period in my life when I was studying for my ATCL or LTCL in speech.

'My Last Duchess' by Robert Browning is very old fashioned, but the cynicism and studied cruelty of the Duke has made it a memorable one for me.

With best wishes,

Yours sincerely,

Dame Silvia Cartwright

My Last Duchess

Ferrara

That's my last Duchess painted on the wall,
Looking as if she were alive. I call
That piece a wonder, now; Frà Pandolf's hands
Worked busily a day, and there she stands.
Will't please you sit and look at her? I said
'Frà Pandolf' by design, for never read
Strangers like you that pictured countenance,
The depth and passion of its earnest glance,
But to myself they turned (since none puts by
The curtain I have drawn for you, but I)

And seemed as they would ask me, if they durst,
How such a glance came there; so, not the first
Are you to turn and ask thus. Sir, 'twas not
her husband's presence only, called that spot
of joy into the Duchess' cheek: perhaps
Frà Pandolf chanced to say 'Her mantle laps
Over my Lady's wrist too much', or 'Paint
Must never hope to reproduce the faint
Half-flush that dies along her throat': such stuff
Was courtesy, she thought, and cause enough
For calling up that spot of joy. She had
A heart — how shall I say? — too soon made glad,
Too easily impressed; she liked whate'er
She looked on, and her looks went everywhere.
Sir, 'twas all one! My favour at her breast,
The dropping of the daylight in the West,
The bough of cherries some officious fool
Broke in the orchard for her, the white mule
She rode with round the terrace — all and each
Would draw from her alike the approving speech,
Or blush, at least. She thanked men, — good! But thanked
Somehow — I know not how — as if she ranked
My gift or a nine-hundred-years-old name
With anybody's gift. Who'd stoop to blame
This sort of trifling? Even had you skill
In speech — (which I have not) — to make your will
Quite clear to such an one, and say, 'Just this
Or that in you disgusts me; here you miss,
Or there exceed the mark' — and if she let
Herself be lessoned so, nor plainly set
Her wits to yours, forsooth, and made excuse,
— E'en then would be some stooping; and I choose
Never to stoop. Oh sir, she smiled, no doubt,
Whene'er I passed her; but who passed without

Much the same smile? This grew; I gave commands;
Then all smiles stopped together. There she stands
As if alive. Will't please you rise? We'll meet
The company below, then. I repeat,
The Count your master's known munificence
Is ample warrant that no just pretence
Of mine for dowry will be disallowed;
Though his fair daughter's self, as I avowed
At starting, is my object. Nay, we'll go
Together down, sir. Notice Neptune, though,
Taming a sea-horse, thought a rarity,
Which Claus of Innsbruck cast in bronze for me!

ROBERT BROWNING

Mike Chunn

MUSICIAN, FOUNDING MEMBER OF SPLIT ENZ AND CITIZEN BAND,
CEO – THE PLAY IT STRANGE TRUST

Dear Libby,

My father was raised in Greymouth in the '20s and '30s. He loved words and by some means was able to develop a love of poetry. I suspect it was his mother's influence. She knew where to find such books.

Greymouth, in those times, was rugby, racing and beer, and a love for Hilaire Belloc was not something you proclaimed from the rooftops. My father didn't. He sought a profession to ensure stability and became a doctor. A good one at that.

But literature, primarily poetry, was his chief love. And from the age of about 30 he started writing his own poems. We (his children) were vaguely aware of this but only ever saw the humorous ones he gave to our mother. It wasn't until about 10 years ago – he in his 70s – that I discovered a drawer full of poems that he had written. I gathered them all up, said, 'Jerry, can I borrow these?' He said, 'Don't lose them!' and I put them in a book. I made 500 copies.

The first one is titled 'Elegy' and I offer it (with his permission) to your publication.

Jerry is a man of few words. Elegy is not a long poem. But for a father to say these things to his children (to anybody) gives away much of what is beautiful about that man.

All the best,

Mike Chunn

Elegy

No man
Leaves nothing behind.
Centuries hence,
Even the childless
Have disturbed a stone a nerve
To change
The exact balance of things.
Somewhere, somehow, a remote
And unconnected life is stirred.

The farrier who shod the prince's horse
Enabled him to reach the castle moat
Before the Sorcerer had raised the drawbridge —
And the girl's reply
Led to the happy ending
Led to the wedding on the lawn,
To the filial quarrels
And the civil wars
And young love sundered.

Each man touches,
To what effect he knows not,
The garment of God.

JERRY CHUNN

Belinda Clark

SECRETARY FOR JUSTICE

Dear Cleo,

My father, George Clark, passed away in 1980 — over 25 years ago — and this poem by Alfred Tennyson was a favourite of his.

George joined the British Navy in World War II and served as an officer on escort ships in the North Atlantic. Although the war experience was cruel, a deep and abiding love of the sea remained with him all his life. He often talked of the majesty and mystery of the sea and loved poems and stories about it. 'Crossing the Bar' was a real sailor's poem to him.

Maybe he had a portent that he would 'not see old bones' (as they used to say), as he often recited this poem, declaiming its last line — 'When I have crost the bar' — in contemplation of his own crossing and remembering those who had crossed before.

To hear or see it again is bitter-sweet, as I see in my mind's eye George reading this poem.

Best wishes for the project.

Kind regards,

Belinda Clark

Crossing the Bar

Sunset and evening star,
    And one clear call for me!
And may there be no moaning of the bar,
    When I put out to sea,

But such a tide as moving seems asleep,
    Too full for sound and foam,
When that which drew from out the boundless deep
    Turns again home.

Twilight and evening bell,
    And after that the dark!
And may there be no sadness of farewell,
    When I embark;

For tho' from out our bourne of Time and Place
    The flood may bear me far,
I hope to see my Pilot face to face
    When I have crost the bar.

ALFRED, LORD TENNYSON

Helen Clark

PRIME MINISTER OF NEW ZEALAND

Dear Libby,

'Kubla Khan' captured my imagination when it was part of the English curriculum during my secondary school days.

As recited verse, it had a cadence which made it relatively easy to memorise.

As written verse it was a delight to read, with its rich prose exploring the outer perimeter of the imagination.

'Kubla Khan' speaks of a magical place akin to a paradise – where great rivers, caves, forests and rocks provide a setting reminiscent of New Zealand's wild, natural beauty.

While there is no reason whatsoever to believe that early knowledge of our country helped Coleridge compose this poem – indeed many attribute it to an opium-induced hallucination – nonetheless his words paint a picture which we can relate to across culture and place.

Helen Clark

Sir Geoffrey Palmer

LAW COMMISSION PRESIDENT, FORMER PRIME MINISTER

Dear Shika and Libby,

My favourite poem is 'Kubla Khan' by Samuel Taylor Coleridge.

This poem is beautifully evocative and mysterious. It is impossible to imagine it written in prose. It contains a sense of foreboding, but also glimpses of hope and a spiritual uplift. When I was a student at university studying English, I used to read it aloud to my wife to be, Margaret. It remains my favourite poem more than 40 years on.

Yours sincerely,

Geoffrey Palmer

Kubla Khan

In Xanadu did Kubla Khan
A stately pleasure-dome decree:
Where Alph, the sacred river, ran
Through caverns measureless to man
    Down to a sunless sea.
So twice five miles of fertile ground
With walls and towers were girdled round:
And there were gardens bright with sinuous rills,
Where blossomed many an incense-bearing tree;
And here were forests ancient as the hills,
Enfolding sunny spots of greenery.

But oh! that deep romantic chasm which slanted
Down the green hill athwart a cedarn cover!
A savage place! as holy and enchanted
As e'er beneath a waning moon was haunted
By woman wailing for her demon-lover!
And from this chasm, with ceaseless turmoil seething,
As if this earth in fast thick pants were breathing,
A mighty fountain momently was forced:
Amid whose swift half-intermitted burst
Huge fragments vaulted like rebounding hail,
Or chaffy grain beneath the thresher's flail:
And 'mid these dancing rocks at once and ever
It flung up momently the sacred river.
Five miles meandering with a mazy motion
Through wood and dale the sacred river ran,
Then reached the caverns measureless to man,
And sank in tumult to a lifeless ocean:
And 'mid this tumult Kubla heard from far
Ancestral voices prophesying war!

The shadow of the dome of pleasure
Floated midway on the waves;
Where was heard the mingled measure
From the fountain and the caves.
It was a miracle of rare device,
A sunny pleasure-dome with caves of ice!

A damsel with a dulcimer
In a vision once I saw:
It was an Abyssinian maid,
And on her dulcimer she played,
Singing of Mount Abora.
Could I revive within me
Her symphony and song,
To such a deep delight 'twould win me,
That with music loud and long,
I would build that dome in air,
That sunny dome! those caves of ice!
And all who heard should see them there,
And all should cry, Beware! Beware!
His flashing eyes, his floating hair!
Weave a circle round him thrice,
And close your eyes with holy dread,
For he on honey-dew hath fed,
And drunk the milk of Paradise.

SAMUEL TAYLOR COLERIDGE

James Coleman

PRESENTER, RADIO LIVE

Dear Libby,

Attached is a poem by my mum, written following the birth of my son (her first grandson). I love it because I can't read it without emotion welling up inside me, and because I know the words are so heartfelt. It is my favourite poem.

Kind regards,

James

Boy

To Archie, with love from Grannie,
October 2005 (before you were named).

I won't forget
The little-boy look on your father's face —
His Christmas morning brown dancing eyes
The result of some magic.
Nor the look —
Half-proud, half-searching my approval
When he first showed me
The miracle of you.
And your mother's soft smile —
Her delight and pride in you determined to wrap
The awe-fulness of birth
And put it gently away.
Faintly etched on them
Was the heart-bulging hugeness of family,
A love of early birdsong —

A New Wisdom.
And you — only, most perfectly — six days old.

ELIZABETH COLEMAN

Sandra Coney

FEMINIST, WRITER, AUCKLAND REGIONAL COUNCILLOR

Dear Cleo,

Thank you for your invitation which has caused me much thought!

I came across my chosen poem when studying the romantic poets as a pupil at Auckland Girls' Grammar School – indeed, I am going to have to confess that my edition of the collected work of John Keats is clearly stamped 'This book is the property of Auckland Girls' Grammar School', an injunction I obviously ignored. Interestingly, the book was purchased at Progressive Books in Darby Street, which was a radical learning ground for students such as myself in the 1960s. A surprising place for venerable old AGGS to buy its books!

I can still recite Keats's sonnet by heart. The message that went deep with me as a young woman on the cusp of adult life in the early '60s, was to get on with life, to be true to yourself. To set important goals, and not be side-tracked by seductive, but ephemeral and ultimately unimportant attractions that might tempt you in your passage through life.

Writing and literature has always been central to my life, and I cling to the belief that the expression of ideas, the reasoned argument, holds the power to make a difference.

Keats's imagery captured my imagination at the age of 15 and has held it all these decades: the books packed full of ripe grain, the imponderable drama and mystery of the night sky.

It is a young person's poem, encapsulating the potential of a life fully lived, even if brief. Now that I am over 60, I think

Keats's declaration of self-reliance and personal integrity is still as relevant as it was all those years ago.

Regards,

Sandra Coney

Sonnet

When I have fears that I may cease to be
    Before my pen has glean'd my teeming brain,
Before high-piled books, in charactery,
    Hold like rich garners the full ripen'd grain;
When I behold, upon the night's starr'd face,
    Huge cloudy symbols of a high romance,
And think that I may never live to trace
    Their shadows, with the magic hand of chance;
And when I feel, fair creature of an hour,
    That I shall never look upon thee more,
Never have relish in the faery power
    Of unreflecting love; – then on the shore
Of the wide world I stand alone, and think
    Till love and fame to nothingness do sink.

JOHN KEATS

Max Cryer

BROADCASTER, ENTERTAINER

Dear Libby

As a young man, I taught English to lads training in industrial subjects — and not geared towards academic matters. I quickly learned that although they did not have the skills I brought, they certainly had skills which I had not: metal-casting, woodwork, engine maintenance etc. A pleasing respect grew between us. For ever after I have been careful not to assess values of a person or group based simply on what I can do myself.

Hence I feel sympathy for Baxter's 'Farmhand' — a man whose hands could tie knots, sink fence-posts, ease cows in calving, plough a straight furrow . . . but who felt he didn't have the skill to twirl girls onto the dance floor.

It would have been the girls' loss.

Max Cryer

Farmhand

You will see him light a cigarette
At the hall door careless, leaning back
Against the wall, or telling some new joke
To a friend, or looking out into the secret night.

But always his eyes turn
To the dance floor and the girls drifting like flowers
Before the music that tears
Slowly in his mind an old wound open.

His red sunburnt face and hairy hands
Were not made for dancing or love-making
But rather the earth wave breaking
To the plough, and crops slow-growing as his mind.

He has no girl to run her fingers through
His sandy hair, and giggle at his side
When Sunday couples walk. Instead
He has his awkward hopes, his envious dreams to yarn to.

But ah in harvest watch him
Forking stooks, effortless and strong —
Or listening like a lover to the song
Clear, without fault, of a new tractor engine.

JAMES K. BAXTER

Graeme Dingle

WRITER, ADVENTURER, YOUTH ADVOCATE

Hi Geraldine,

Attached is my favourite piece of poetry – apparently written by a young Spitfire pilot shortly before he died while training during World War Two. It always brings a lump to my throat when I read it.

Very best wishes,

Graeme Dingle ONZM, MBE

High Flight

Oh! I have slipped the surly bonds of Earth
And danced the sky on laughter-silvered wings;
Sunward I've climbed and joined the tumbling mirth
Of sun-split clouds and done a hundred things
You have not dreamed of – wheeled and soared and swung
High in the sunlit silence. Hov'ring there,
I've chased the shouting wind along, and flung
My eager craft through footless halls of air . . .

Up, up the long, delirious, burning blue
I've topped the wind-swept heights with easy grace –
Where never lark nor ever eagle flew –
And, while with silent lifting mind I've trod
The high untrespassed sanctity of space,
Put out my hand, and touched the face of God.

JOHN GILLESPIE MAGEE, JR

Dave Dobbyn

MUSICIAN, SONGWRITER

Hi Esther and Libby,

Great to hear about *Dear to Me*. I'm attaching J.K. Baxter's 'Song of the Years' (1958) which leapt up at me from his *Selected Poems*.

Having endured years of alcoholism myself, after reading this poem I was drawn to its redemptive power. Baxter describes himself as 'singing on the gallows cart' and having the 'aardvark and the onager [ass] stabled at my sepulchre'. Having him name his craziness like that rang with my own sense of deliverance and indeed salvation. It was as if I had always known there was a song to tell my story and that day I found it in J.K.B.'s lines. Powerful stuff is the word. His will ring on forever for me.

All the best.

Warm regards,

Dave Dobbyn

Song of the Years

When from my mother's womb I came
Disputandum was my name.

Weeping hoping threatening
Beyond myself I had no king.

I drew in with each hour's breath
The grey dust of the second death.

When my childhood days were spent
To Venus I grew suppliant.

Little tremors woke and died
Within the mountain of my pride.

Singing on the gallows cart
Created beauty held my heart.

The aardvark and the onager
Were stabled at my sepulchre.

In that deep den the King of bliss
Broke my heart and gave me His.

'This for your doom and penance take,
Be merry always for My sake.'

He gave me a white stone to bear
With my true name written there.

Without end I will say,
Laus tibi, Domine!

JAMES K. BAXTER

Lynley Dodd

CHILDREN'S AUTHOR AND ILLUSTRATOR

Dear Shika,

I have many favourites so it has been difficult to choose. However I have finally settled on Walter de la Mare's 'The Listeners', a favourite from childhood. The poem has always had a spine-tingling resonance for me and re-reading it evokes strong memories of the little one-room country school where I heard it for the first time as an eight-year-old.

Lynley Dodd

The Listeners

Is there anybody there?' said the Traveller,
    Knocking on the moonlit door;
And his horse in the silence champed the grasses
    Of the forest's ferny floor:
And a bird flew up out of the turret,
    Above the Traveller's head:
And he smote upon the door again a second time;
    'Is there anybody there?' he said.
But no one descended to the Traveller;
    No head from the leaf-fringed sill
Leaned over and looked into his grey eyes,
    Where he stood perplexed and still.
But only a host of phantom listeners
    That dwelt in the lone house then
Stood listening in the quiet of the moonlight
    To that voice from the world of men:

Stood thronging the faint moonbeams on the dark stair,
    That goes down to the empty hall,
Hearkening in an air stirred and shaken
    By the lonely Traveller's call.
And he felt in his heart their strangeness,
    Their stillness answering his cry,
While his horse moved, cropping the dark turf,
    'Neath the starred and leafy sky;
For he suddenly smote on the door, even
    Louder, and lifted his head:–
'Tell them I came, and no one answered,
    That I kept my word,' he said.
Never the least stir made the listeners,
    Though every word he spake
Fell echoing through the shadowiness of the still house
    From the one man left awake:
Ay, they heard his foot upon the stirrup,
    And the sound of iron on stone,
And how the silence surged softly backward,
    When the plunging hoofs were gone.

WALTER DE LA MARE

Graeme Downes

FOUNDING MEMBER OF THE VERLAINES, SENIOR LECTURER IN
CONTEMPORARY ROCK MUSIC, UNIVERSITY OF OTAGO

Dear Geraldine,

Always had a soft spot for this one. It was probably my first
introduction to New Zealand poetry outside of school (to which
I had paid little attention, as often tends to happen in school —
Baxter, to my eternal shame, left me cold at 14). It was possibly
at the first of the Sam Hunt/Gary McCormick road shows that
I became acquainted with it. The recital was at the Fortune
Theatre, an old church, with the sun streaming through the
stained-glass windows. And there was this lurching, barking
man spellbinding an audience of I can't remember how many,
with these succinct little vignettes, words like fine whisky
distilled from the grain of existence. I bought the book he
was promoting at the time but doubt I would have forged the
attachment to this poem in particular without the delivery, the
music of it, poetry not in books but in flesh. It's true that Sam's
style of delivery can be a bit samey such that a John Gadsby
can lovingly take the piss. So be it. But when I hear or
remember that broken bell of a voice it's this poem that
often comes to mind.

Graeme Downes

My Father Today

They buried him today
up Schnapper Rock Road,
my father in cold clay.

A heavy south wind towed
the drape of light away.
Friends, men met on the road,

stood round in that dumb way
men stand when lost for words.
There was nothing to say.

I heard the bitchy chords
of magpies in an old-man
pine . . . *My* old man, he's worlds

away – call it Heaven –
no man so elegantly
dressed. His last afternoon,

staring out to sea,
he nods off in his chair.
He wonders what the

yelling's all about up there.
They just about explode!
And now, these magpies here

up Schnapper Rock Road . . .
They buried him in clay.
He was a heavy load,

my dead father today.

SAM HUNT

Brian Easton

ECONOMIST, SOCIAL STATISTICIAN, PUBLIC POLICY ANALYST

Dear Esther,

A copy of 'Secular Litany' by M.K. (Michael Keith) Joseph is on the notice board above my desk as I write. It was put there, many years ago, because of the couplet

> That we may avoid distinction and exception
> Worship the mean, cultivate the mediocre

especially as a warning against cultivating mediocrity. Not everyone can be top of the class, but no one need be mediocre, which my thesaurus couples with 'banal', 'indifferent', 'pedestrian', 'undistinguished' and 'uninspired'. It is about an attitude of mind, to try to excel within the limitations that God gave each of us.

But you can't have a poem sitting up there for as long as this one has been, without pondering on its broader theme. From today's perspective — 50 years after it was written — it describes a strange world, for almost all the images are now obsolete. Sure, there are still the All Blacks and excellence is often lower on the intellectual agenda than the safe, the conventional wisdom, and the politically correct (although less so in some areas such as the arts and sport). But hardly anything else in the poem applies today. What New Zealander would ask of Saint Holidays to defend us 'from all foreigners with their unintelligible cooking' and even from 'barbecues'? Did we once reject 'kermesse [fairs and bazaars] and carnival, high day and festival'?

I wonder how many people today would know that a litany is a series of religious petitions? When the poem was written, people attended church services and would be aware of the ritual. Joseph, a regular church-goer, could see those practices were dying. Today they are dead for most of us – known only to a minority.

So it is a list poem. You could change some of the examples – even leave them out – and while the poetic structure might be damaged, the sentiment would not. I have wondered whether the list could be modernised – not by me – for I have none of Joseph's poetic talent. Sure we have our icons, but often they are a fashion soon forgotten. There would be less collective agreement about what they were. We are a more diverse society.

Joseph is, of course, satirising the early post-war attitudes as dull, philistine and conforming, but not so unrecognisably that the poem was ignored. It was even anthologised. The adult world it describes is on the edge of my childhood memories, even if it seems a long way from the world in which I now live.

This led me to ponder: what are the cultural commonalities between the New Zealand of that time and today? I even wrote a *Listener* (January 2005) column about it to illustrate the problem of cultural continuities – of how one generation connects with another – and to ask what really is at the heart of being a New Zealander.

It becomes more personal when I reflect on my father, who died a few years back. Like everyone else, Dad was not entirely in the mainstream, but the world which he came from is the one Joseph portrays. So how do I connect to Dad – other than through filial affection, our shared experiences and love? Did we have the same culture? And will my children, when they get to my age, be posed with the same problem? Are they already?

Towards the end of his life Dad became quite grumpy about social changes which were transforming his world. 'Secular

Litany' illustrates the extent of the transformation. And it must be happening to my world too – perhaps even faster. So when I face a new world, say, of mobile phones or hip hop, I think of the transformation in the past and try to tolerate the one going on today. After all, the poem is about a society unwilling to tolerate diversity. I hope we do better today.

For despite talking about a world of long ago and long gone, the poem has a lot of my life story in it. Which is why I still keep it up on my notice-board, above me as I write.

Thank you for the opportunity to contribute to the project.

Brian

Secular Litany

That we may never lack two Sundays in a week
One to rest and one to play
That we may worship in the liturgical drone
Of the race commentator and the radio raconteur
That we may avoid distinction and exception
Worship the mean, cultivate the mediocre
Live in a state house, raise forcibly-educated children
Receive family benefits, and standard wages and a pension
And rest in peace in a state crematorium
    Saint Allblack
    Saint Monday Raceday
    Saint Stabilisation
      Pray for us.

From all foreigners, with their unintelligible cooking
From the vicious habit of public enjoyment
From kermesse and carnival, high day and festival
From pubs, cafés, bullfights and barbecues

From Virgil and vintages, fountains and fresco-painting
From afterthought and apperception
From tragedy, from comedy
And from the arrow of God
    Saint Anniversaryday
    Saint Arborday
    Saint Labourday
      Defend us.

When the bottles are empty
And the keg runs sour
And the cinema is shut and darkened
And the radio gone up in smoke
And the sports-ground flooded
When the tote goes broke
And the favourite scratches
And the brass bands are silenced
And the car is rusted by the roadside
    Saint Fathersday
    Saint Mothersday
    Saint Happybirthday
      Have mercy on us.

And for your petitioner, poor little Jim,
    Saint Hocus
    Saint Focus
    Saint Bogus
    And Saint Billy Bungstarter
      Have mercy on him.

M.K. JOSEPH

David Eggleton

WRITER, POET

Dear Shika,

The poem I have chosen is 'I'm Nobody! Who are you?' by
Emily Dickinson. It seems simple, like part of a conversation,
but there's a lot going on in it.

Emily Dickinson's poems are endlessly quotable; the best of
them are such marvels of metrical intricacy and lively imagery
that they almost seem to possess beating hearts. Born in 1830
in Amherst, Massachusetts into a devout Christian family,
Emily herself was the odd one out: she teased and mocked
and was a religious doubter. She was a creature of paradox;
despite having a high-spirited personality, she chose to live
as a recluse, rarely leaving her family home, and she never
married.

She wrote constantly – her collected works amount to around
1800 poems – but she published almost nothing in her lifetime.
Her writings were discovered in her room after her death. She
was an independent thinker and one reason she chose not to
publish was that she was an innovator who created her own
way of writing.

Part sceptic, part ecstatic, she has been called America's
greatest religious poet and one of the greatest woman poets
ever. One of the poems of hers that I most like is a kind of
comical throwaway poem that's also profound – as reverberant
as an echo. It's a strange attractor poem with its mirror
imagery, and it's also a kind of question and answer riddle
written in clear but jabbing phrases. She's written some
wonderful poems about animals – the cat, the bird, the rat,

the bee, the butterfly – but I like here the mention of the frog. It's a funny poem about anonymity, but there's a lot of different emotions running through it: it's sardonic and defiant, but also maybe a bit envious and bitter. Whatever, its complexity reveals her as a true successor to William Shakespeare – his soul sister, perhaps.

Best regards,

David Eggleton

I'm Nobody! Who are you?

I'm Nobody! Who are you?
Are you – Nobody – Too?
Then there's a pair of us!
Don't tell! they'd advertise – you know!

How dreary – to be – Somebody!
How public – like a Frog –
To tell one's name – the livelong June –
To an admiring Bog!

EMILY DICKINSON

Riemke Ensing

POET

Dear Libby,

This is not necessarily the 'favourite' poem you requested.
For that I'd go first to Yeats and T.S. Eliot and perhaps the
wonderful eccentricity and exuberance of 'Glory be to God
for dappled things'. There are so many 'favourite' poems I'd
find it difficult to come up with just the one.

In the context of this particular anthology however, Ahmed
Zaoui's poem 'is a vital presence on our poetry radar'. Emma
Neale, as editor of the online project *Best New Zealand Poems
2004*, selected it as 'the most important poem for its role as a
nexus of politics and aesthetics . . . where the cry of the soul
is brought up against the hard wall of poem as technical
artifact, an object made in language, a social construct'.

I first met Ahmed Zaoui in the Auckland Central Remand
Prison. His lawyer Deborah Manning had asked me to help
interpret some poems he had written during his period of
confinement. We gathered, with Jassine Belkamel and
Mohammed Felgouma – both Arab speakers, scholars, and
friends of Ahmed – first in the waiting area, then in the
visiting hall, to work out how we might best present the
original in English. I already had Tarek Cherkaoui's two very
differing English translations – one in rhyming couplets.

It was very strange to be working on a poem in that appalling
environment, but oddly we soon found ourselves completely
focused – not just on the poem, but also in raising Ahmed's
spirits. The two men were particularly adept at this. They were
impressed by the allusions, the symbolism and the double

entendres but were constantly falling about laughing, especially at Ahmed's use of the words 'my love', for which they ribbed him mercilessly. Of course it was all a game – an attempt to keep him from despair in that desolate and sunless place.

I personally found going into the Auckland Central Remand Prison a daunting and terrifying experience even though I was only a visitor and knew I could (theoretically, at least) get out. Imagine being incarcerated in solitary confinement in Paremoremo – a maximum-security prison – *for almost a year, without having a charge brought against you.* And this in New Zealand – a land that prides itself on its human-rights record.

Ahmed Zaoui, who has become a friend, is at the centre of an ongoing struggle for freedom and justice. Amnesty International took up his case. The United Nations issued a reprimand to the New Zealand Government because of the conditions under which he was detained. What's happened to *Habeus Corpus* and all those little conventions that constitute the rule of law in this country? Seems like we've gone the road of Guantanamo Bay.

I read this poem at an Amnesty International fund-raising event in 2004. By that time Ahmed had been in prison for almost two years. Despite having been declared a genuine refugee in August 2003, he is still not 'out of the woods'. On bail, he awaits the 'review' of his 'Security Risk Certificate'. Due to ongoing delays in the legal process, it looks likely that by the time this book is launched on Montana Poetry Day in July 2007, Ahmed Zaoui (and his family in exile overseas) will still be waiting in a Kafkaesque trial for their lives, which effectively began here in December 2002.

Riemke Ensing

He Will Come Back, the One I'm Waiting for

In the dream, I am travelling.
I am walking in a beautiful forest.
Suddenly a man calls out to me. He is a woodsman.
He recognises me as a stranger and reaches to shake my hand.
I am delighted, thinking we are friends, but he stares at me,
rigid, like wood. He takes spectacles from his pocket
and peers more closely. 'You are a foreigner', he says,
'I accuse you! You will die,

    but it will have nothing to do with me.'
He glares at me again. His face a grimace. 'Don't worry',
    he says,
'We will prepare for you a coffin and a shroud.'

Miraculously then, birds appear. They surround the woodsman
    and sing;
'Leave him alone. He is of the people. He is the liberator.
    Let him go!'
But the axeman shouts; 'He is a liar. Hear me, people,
    he's a liar. He must die!'
I wake up from the dream on notes of music. My love hears
    my cries of fear.
'Will I return, will I return?' She answers; 'Yes, you will
come back like the migrating bird travelling always home.
We will pick dates together when the sun shines and showers
make rainbows.'

Then I scream. I am wracked with pain and tears.
    My body an agony.
My mind a cauldron of fire. 'But when will I return?
    How long must I wait?
    How long? How long?'

AHMED ZAOUI

Jacqueline Fahey

ARTIST

Dear Cleo,

Since I was a child I have loved this Irish street ballad, 'Johnny, I Hardly Knew Ye'.

The music is the same as in 'When Johnny Comes Marching Home Again, Hurroo! Hurroo!' from the American Civil War, and as 'Johnny, I Hardly Knew Ye' pre-dates that ballad we have to assume that the Americans borrowed the music and changed the words. Perhaps the Irish words were a little too close to the bone. They are hard, simple and energetic, they go for clarity, and clarity is the lasting quality of Gaelic poetry. After the Battle of the Boyne young men from Ireland were recruited into armies all over Europe, from Russia to Spain. Of all the pains Ireland suffered, the greatest of all was to see her young men go to Europe as cannon fodder for foreign princes. These were called the Wild Geese because the young men's departure was as fixed in the calendar of Ireland's seasons as the departure of the wild geese. This street ballad could equally apply to the poor boys of the South in the United States who are, at this very moment, coerced into a brutal war. Some come home again without a leg, an arm, or an eye.

Good luck with your project, it is important.

Yours sincerely,

Jacqueline Fahey

Johnny, I Hardly Knew Ye

While going the road to sweet Athy,
        Hurroo! hurroo!
While going the road to sweet Athy,
        Hurroo! hurroo!
While going the road to sweet Athy,
A stick in my hand and a drop in my eye,
A doleful damsel I heard cry:–
        'Och, Johnny, I hardly knew ye!

'With drums and guns and guns and drums
        The enemy nearly slew ye,
        My darling dear, you look so queer,
Och, Johnny, I hardly knew ye!

'Where are your eyes that looked so mild?
        Hurroo! hurroo!
Where are your eyes that looked so mild?
        Hurroo! hurroo!
Where are your eyes that looked so mild,
When my poor heart you first beguiled?
Why did you run from me and the child?
        Och, Johnny, I hardly knew ye!
With drums, etc.

'Where are the legs with which you run?
        Hurroo! hurroo!
Where are the legs with which you run?
        Hurroo! hurroo!
Where are the legs with which you run,
When you went to carry a gun?–
Indeed, your dancing days are done!
        Och, Johnny, I hardly knew ye!

With drums, etc.

'It grieved my heart to see you sail,
        Hurroo! hurroo!
It grieved my heart to see you sail,
        Hurroo! hurroo!
It grieved my heart to see you sail,
Though from my heart you took leg bail, —
Like a cod you're doubled up head and tail.
        Och, Johnny, I hardly knew ye!
With drums, etc.

'You haven't an arm and you haven't a leg,
        Hurroo! hurroo!
You haven't an arm and you haven't a leg,
        Hurroo! hurroo!
You haven't an arm and you haven't a leg,
You're an eyeless, noseless, chickenless egg;
You'll have to be put in a bowl to beg:
        Och, Johnny, I hardly knew ye!
With drums, etc.

'I'm happy for to see you home,
        Hurroo! hurroo!
I'm happy for to see you home,
        Hurroo! hurroo!
I'm happy for to see you home,
All from the island of Sulloon,
So low in flesh, so high in bone,
        Och, Johnny, I hardly knew ye!
With drums, etc.

'But sad as it is to see you so,
        Hurroo! hurroo!

But sad as it is to see you so,
        Hurroo! hurroo!
But sad as it is to see you so,
And to think of you now as an object of woe,
Your Peggy'll still keep ye on as her beau;
        Och, Johnny, I hardly knew ye!

'With drums and guns and guns and drums
        The enemy nearly slew ye,
        My darling dear, you look so queer,
Och, Johnny, I hardly knew ye!'

ANON

Fiona Farrell

NOVELIST, POET

The Lament of the Nun of Beare

Ebb to me!

In old age, the tide turns,
brings back the blood
and I grieve at its coming
yet am glad at the flood.

I am the nun of Beare.
Once my dresses were new.
Now my shift is so thin
my bones show through.

I loved people, not riches,
when I was alive.
Loved their wide plains
over which I could drive.

Swift chariots I had
and horses fleet.
*(Bless the kings who
gave them to me!)*
Now they hand me a
penny whenever we meet.

My body is fearful
of this Son of God
and the judgement
he'll make when I'm
under the sod.

Bony my hands now
that once touched
splendid men.
Too bony to rise over
sweet boys again!

Girls laugh and delight
at the coming of spring.
But I, an old woman,
have sorrows to sing.

No wedding lamb for my table,
I pour no good ale.
My hair grey and scanty
beneath a white veil.

Once I wore coloured
veils over my hair.
Now my veil is white,
and I no longer care.

Nothing old do I envy
but Femin's wide plains,
so fair. Storms rage –
yet they spring back:
fresh-cheeked,
golden-haired.

Tonight in the darkness
the winter waves roar
No king's son nor slave's
son will visit my door.

I am cold. Wear a shawl
to sit in the sun.
Winter comes in to smother.
Youth's summer is done.

I was wanton in my youth
and I'm glad I was bold!
If I'd been more cautious
I'd still sit here: old

in my ancient cloak —
when the bare hills' covering
is the fine icy cloak
flung down by the King.

God help me! Whose bright eyes
to candle feast were the spark,
now dim in a wooden church,
decayed in the dark.

Mead and wine with kings
I drank in my day.
Now I sit with old women
drinking water and whey.

May I drink from this cup!
May my blood turn from rage!
May I accept as God's will
This chilly old age!

May I accept as my cloak
this grey hair that on me
grows through my skin as
lichen on a gnarled tree.

My right eye snatched from me
as payment and due.
To complete the transaction,
my left eye taken too.

The flood wave and the swift ebb.
What is brought to your hand,
the ebb draws from you.
This, I understand:

Flood wave and swift ebb.

I know these to be so.

I have fed all from my pantry.
I have never said 'no'.

I have taken in strangers,
I have done my best.
Now the Son of Man
is my only guest.

Happy the island
in the midst of the sea,
for flood follows ebb.
But not for me.

Sad my dwelling and
empty, on this bare day.

I must learn from
my sadness:

that all ebbs away.

UNKNOWN IRISH POET
(English version: Fiona Farrell)

Dear Va,

This is my version of 'The Lament of the Hag/Nun of Beare'. It
was probably composed by an anonymous Irish poet in the fifth
or sixth century, and first appears in a written form in the tenth
century.

It has been variously interpreted (as political allegory for
instance) but to me it speaks as a howl against change and
death. The speaker is a cailleach – an Irish word that can mean
'nun' (a Christian nun) but also 'hag', meaning the pre-Christian
crone or goddess in her winter phase before her rebirth in
spring.

I love everything about this poem, beginning with the
physicality of the first verse: that the woman has blood again,
in old age. (Now she'd probably be prescribed HRT.) She recalls
her life as a priestess in pre-Christian Ireland – a prestigious
role in a society whose faith for thousands of years had placed
a goddess at the pinnacle of the pantheon, not a male god.
This woman has mixed with kings and driven about the fertile
plains in her own chariot, in brilliantly coloured clothing.

But a new faith has arrived: the Christian faith preached by forceful, organisational men like Patrick. The old woman has been compelled to deal with the realities of social change, age, irrelevancy and loss of power.

I'm 60 this year. I've watched the dismantling and undermining of the socialist and feminist legacy that gave me freedom and health and an education. My great-grandmother couldn't write, but I make my living as a writer: the fortunate beneficiary of political changes that for just a split second in a couple of thousand years of human history permitted me, a working-class female, to write and publish books that other women were actually able to read. A kind of childish machismo flavours this era: 24-hour rugby, rape as nightly fodder for entertainment on prime-time tv, a general consensus that it's tolerable for the strongest to grab what they can while children subsist in poverty in this rich and beautiful land. I feel out of step with the era and like the nun/hag: angry.

The nun/hag in this poem has moved from the rich plains to Beara, a peninsula in southwest Ireland that juts out into the wild waters of the Atlantic, its big bare hills supposedly created when they dropped like eggs from the apron of the old cailleach. I visited it while I was living in Ireland in 2006. I wanted to see a stone near Ardgroom that is called 'The Hag of Beara'. It's not big or obvious. It doesn't feature in the guide books. It's just a tubby lump of bubbly volcanic rock in an otherwise granite landscape, standing all by itself overlooking the sea.

A summer afternoon. A little fishing boat smack smacking its way out to sea in the bay below. The drone of a tractor from a field where some men were cutting hay. People had left things on the hag's crevices: rosary beads, ear rings, hair clips, coins. I left my pen.

I love this poem's age and the way its voice carries down the centuries. I love what it says, and I love the way it is said, the imagery of tide and ebb, women's blood tied to the moon and the tide, the way we are part of nature at the most fundamental level. It is just absolutely beautiful.

Fiona Farrell

Otis Frizzell

ARTIST

Hey Libby,

My mother and father used this wee verse to help me overcome my fear of the dark when I was very young. I remember when I first really heard it and I've remembered it ever since.

My family and I used to spend the summer holidays camping with friends in a pine forest in Pakiri. It was a 15-minute walk to the beach over the sand dunes. One evening Mum, Dad and I took a walk to the beach and it was dark by the time we headed back to camp. I was okay on the dunes because it was lit by the moon and stars, but when we got to the manuka before the pine forest we walked into a soupy blackness. The sounds of the bush and the virtual blackness freaked me out completely until Mum told me the poem. Even now, at 35, if I ever feel any rush of anxiety at being in the dark in an unfamiliar place, I can say it to myself and it kinda chills me out.

Otis Frizzell

Bump!

Things that go 'bump!' in the night,
Should not really give one a fright.
It's the hole in each ear
That lets in the fear,
That, and the absence of light!

SPIKE MILLIGAN

Maurice Gee

AUTHOR

Dear Shika,

I have a swag of poems I love, any of which could qualify as favourite. I've chosen this one because I've seen the Danish bog people and know that Seamus Heaney has described Tollund Man perfectly. In part two he moves beyond the sacrificial victim to enter other but still specific areas of grief and pain. It's a perfect poem – perfect in expression, in its widening out and in its return to the personal. I hope you won't find it too painful. Although the last stanza can't be read as expressing acceptance it brings us to a quiet end.

Yours sincerely,

Maurice Gee

The Tollund Man

I
Some day I will go to Aarhus
To see his peat-brown head,
The mild pods of his eye-lids,
His pointed skin cap.

In the flat country nearby
Where they dug him out,
His last gruel of winter seeds
Caked in his stomach,

Naked except for
The cap, noose and girdle,
I will stand a long time.
Bridegroom to the goddess,

She tightened her torc on him
And opened her fen,
Those dark juices working
Him to a saint's kept body,

Trove of the turfcutters'
Honeycombed workings.
Now his stained face
Reposes at Aarhus.

II
I could risk blasphemy,
Consecrate the cauldron bog
Our holy ground and pray
Him to make germinate

The scattered, ambushed
Flesh of labourers,
Stockinged corpses
Laid out in the farmyards,

Tell-tale skin and teeth
Flecking the sleepers
Of four young brothers, trailed
For miles along the lines.

III
Something of his sad freedom
As he rode the tumbril
Should come to me, driving,
Saying the names

Tollund, Grauballe, Nebelgard,
Watching the pointing hands
Of country people,
Not knowing their tongue.

Out there in Jutland
In the old man-killing parishes
I will feel lost,
Unhappy and at home.

SEAMUS HEANEY

Jenny Gibbs

PHILANTHROPIST, ART PATRON AND COLLECTOR

Dear Shika,

I think what your group is doing is great so I will happily participate. I am also a member of Amnesty (Freedom Foundation) and have been for many years. Also my daughters Mandi Gibbs and Emma Gibbs both went to AGGS.

I have enclosed a copy of my poem, 'Hotere' by Hone Tuwhare. The reason I have chosen it is that it relates to two wonderful New Zealanders, both of whom I know, who are both warm creative caring people, both Maori, both getting on in years, both laugh a lot and both love eating muttonbirds!

The Tuwhare poem is talking about a series of Hotere paintings which I know and love and which consist of fine lines either vertical, stacked horizontal or a fine circle, all on a shiny black lacquered paint – very apparently simple but as Hone Tuwhare is really saying in the poem, enough to knock your socks off – like 'I'm eclipsed'. I also fell in love with the poem again when I heard Bill Manhire read it.

Best wishes and good luck,

Jenny Gibbs

Hotere

When you offer only three
vertical lines precisely drawn
and set into a dark pool of lacquer
it is a visual kind of starvation:
and even though my eyeballs
roll up and over to peer inside
myself, when I reach the beginning
of your eternity I say instead: hell
let's have another feed of mussels

Like, I have to think about it, man

When you stack horizontal lines
into vertical columns which appear
to advance, recede, shimmer and wave
like exploding packs of cards
I merely grunt and say: well, if it
is not a famine, it's a feast

I have to roll another smoke, man

But when you score a superb orange
circle on a purple thought-base
I shake my head and say: hell, what
is this thing called *aroha*

Like, I'm euchred, man. I'm eclipsed?

HONE TUWHARE

101

Phil Goff

MP FOR MT ROSKILL

Dear Va,

Thank you for asking me to contribute a poem to your *Dear to Me* anthology. I commend you all for your commitment to the aims of Amnesty International.

The poem I have selected is 'The Skeleton of the Great Moa in the Canterbury Museum, Christchurch' by Allen Curnow. I really wanted to choose a work by a New Zealand poet for your anthology and believe that this poem has an important message.

The poem uses the metaphor of the extinct moa to focus the attention of the reader on the issues we all face as New Zealanders, coming to terms with our identity and adapting to life on our 'islands'. The poem has a variety of interpretations but I take it to mean that unless we 'learn the trick of standing upright here' and learn to celebrate our country, we run the risk of becoming locked in the past.

I find the image of a 'huge egg' being 'Found in a thousand pieces, pieced together' very fitting given the huge number of different cultures and nationalities which make up modern New Zealand, and believe that Curnow was optimistic about our ability to come together as a country.

It is pleasing to see a group of young people taking such an interest in international justice and I am sure your fund-raising efforts will be successful.

Please do not hesitate to contact me if I can be of further assistance.

Kind regards,

Hon Phil Goff

The Skeleton of the Great Moa
in the Canterbury Museum, Christchurch

The skeleton of the moa on iron crutches
Broods over no great waste; a private swamp
Was where this tree grew feathers once, that hatches
Its dusty clutch, and guards them from the damp.

Interesting failure to adapt on islands,
Taller but not more fallen than I, who come
Bone to his bone, peculiarly New Zealand's.
The eyes of children flicker round this tomb

Under the skylights, wonder at the huge egg
Found in a thousand pieces, pieced together
But with less patience than the bones that dug
In time deep shelter against ocean weather:

Not I, some child, born in a marvellous year,
Will learn the trick of standing upright here.

ALLEN CURNOW

William Gruar

BLERTA MEMBER, WRITER

Dear Va,

Ostensibly a religious poem, 'On his Blindness' is more an affirmation of man's spirit in overcoming adversity with creativity and inner strength. Milton does not complain about what could be an incarceration inside his own head, but delights in the realisation that he is alive and sentient. The poem is also a classic example of the sonnet form, balanced, rhyming, cogent and eminently available to any reader.

William Gruar

On His Blindness

When I consider how my light is spent
    Ere half my days in this dark world and wide,
    And that one talent which is death to hide
    Lodg'd with me useless, though my soul more bent
To serve therewith my Maker, and present
    My true account, lest he returning chide,
    'Doth God exact day-labour, light denied?'
    I fondly ask. But Patience, to prevent
That murmur, soon replies: 'God doth not need
    Either man's work or his own gifts: who best
    Bear his mild yoke, they serve him best. His state
Is kingly; thousands at his bidding speed
    And post o'er land and ocean without rest:
    They also serve who only stand and wait.'

JOHN MILTON

Nicky Hager

AUTHOR, INVESTIGATIVE JOURNALIST

Dear Esther,

There are lots of poems that I can see are clever or well written but which do not grab me or move me. Then every once in a while one does. 'High Country Weather', by James K. Baxter, is one such poem.

I see this poem as being about the things we have in common and that hold us together: of life and death and our shared land. Even when we have fierce personal or political differences, we still have more in common than not. We still share the same streets and views of distant mountains. These should be a foundation of understanding and respect. At the same time, the beauty of nature gives pleasure and perspective that protect us from becoming bitter or disheartened.

All the best,

Nicky Hager

Elizabeth Hawthorne

ACTOR

Dear Shika,

I chose this poem because:

It is arresting and shocking.

It demands attention.

It requires one to stop.

It seamlessly encompasses the elementary elements of poetry.

Condensed, essential, connecting profundity.

Life and death.

Exquisite beauty. Brevity.

Splendid images of heart expanding dimension evoked with simple, direct language.

A call to one's inner reflective self with a demand to attend the magnificence of creation.

An absolution/forgiveness/recognition of our fragile humanity yet a challenge to the greater self.

At once personal and universal. Intimate and colossal.

I also enjoy the echo from *Hamlet*, 'But, look, the morn, in russet mantle clad':

> Yet see the red-gold cirrus
> Over snow-mountain shine.

The call to look beyond oneself, to stretch, to encompass the greater design.

The exhortation to transcend the domestic and inhabit the epic.

Regards,

Elizabeth Hawthorne

High Country Weather

Alone we are born
 And die alone;
Yet see the red-gold cirrus
 Over snow-mountain shine.

Upon the upland road
 Ride easy, stranger:
Surrender to the sky
 Your heart of anger.

JAMES K. BAXTER

Roger Hall

PLAYWRIGHT

Dear Geraldine,

Fifty lines or less . . . ? Well there goes 'Ode to a Nightingale'.
So does what is currently my favourite poem, Carol Ann
Duffy's 'The Laughter at Stafford Girls' High' because that's 20
pages. Vincent O'Sullivan's 'Don't Knock The Rawleigh's Man'
delighted me so much that soon after reading it, we were
driving through Sanson (I think) and I was determined to visit
the Rawleigh's Man there (who seems to sell from his home
rather than take around a bag that 'flies open like leather
wings').

I have to say that his range of products compared to what
Vince's salesman had to offer was a considerable
disappointment.

Roger Hall

Don't Knock the Rawleigh's Man

Don't knock the Rawleigh's Man
when he opens his case and offers you
mixed spices, curry powder, chilblain
ointment, Ready Relief, brilliantine,
don't say *Not now*, don't think
Piss off, but remember:
think of a hill called Tibi Dabo
behind Barcelona and the legend
that up there Satan
showed J.C. just what he was missing.
What he offered was not simply
the vulgar things – the girls
with buttocks like mounded cream
or enough money in brewery shares
to take a Rotarian's mind off mowing lawns
for octogenarian widows,
or the sort of drink we all know
Vice-Chancellors drink when they drink
with other Vice-Chancellors –
not that but more deftly
the luciferic fingers fondled
buttons nostalgic with little anchors
as in the Mansfield story
and bits of coloured glass from old houses
and variously, these: good punctuation,
unattainable notes, throaty grunts
at bedtime, the nape of the neck
of lovely ladies caught in lamplight
like the perfect compliance of the pitch
in the last over when the last ball
takes the intransigent wicket –
yes, he did. Satan offered those things,

those were the things turned down,
that's how serious it was.
And what was round the corner as we know
was a tree already chopped
waiting to be a cross and a woman
at home rinsing a cloth white as she could
and Joseph of Arimathea still thinking the rock
he had hollowed at phenomenal expense
was going to be his, forever,
not Some Body Else's, for a spell . . .
So when the bag snaps on *your* doorstep,
flies open like leather wings
and you see instead of feathers
the tucked-in jars, the notched tubes,
the salves the spices
the lovely stuff of the flesh,
ask him in, go on, in for a moment.
There's no telling what else he might show you —
what mountain he has in mind
you may cast yourself from,
what price that your hair shimmer
like a diving hawk.

VINCENT O'SULLIVAN

Miranda Harcourt

ACTOR

Dear Lisa,

I discovered this poem recently and it is my new favourite.

In it journalist, novelist, poet Robin Hyde (pen name for Iris Wilkinson) remembers her childhood round the south coast beaches of Wellington — where I live now with my family.

'Close Under Here' is part six of a sequence called 'The Beaches', itself part of a longer cycle published after her death as *Houses By The Sea*.

The poem was completed in 1939, just before she committed suicide in London at the age of 33.

There is such longing in this poem. The bitter-sweet longing of memory — but also sexual longing, bold for the time and still vivid.

There is tension in the writing between the seemingly languid nature of the scene — a sunny day, the hot sand, sparkling water, two lovers — and the thrill and shock of the sex revealed in the very words she chooses ('It wasn't long before they came', 'jerked off', 'Dick, my frock!').

It's like Robin Hyde is smuggling truth past the bleak morality of the time.

We read a lot of male New Zealand poets of the '30s, but not many women. Hyde's life was both tragic and triumphant: solo mother, drug addict, passionate lover, outspoken social critic, godwit . . . She was the first female journalist to report from the front line during the Second Sino–Japanese War; and only escaped from battle at great personal cost.

But Hyde — author of the lyrical autobiographical novel *The Godwits Fly* and the terrifying war novel *Passport To Hell* — knew her own moment. In *A Home in this World* — written while a voluntary patient at Auckland Mental Hospital — she notes, 'I am caught in the hinge of a slowly-opening door, between one age and another. Between the tradition of respectability . . . and the new age'.

Miranda

from **The Beaches**

VI
Close under here, I watched two lovers once,
Which should have been a sin, from what you say:
I'd come to look for prawns, small pale-green ghosts,
Sea-coloured bodies tickling round the pool.
But tide was out then; so I strolled away
And climbed the dunes, to lie here warm, face down,
Watching the swimmers by the jetty-posts
And wrinkling like the bright blue wrinkling bay.
It wasn't long before they came; a fool
Could see they had to kiss; but your pet dunce
Didn't quite know men count on more than that;
And so just lay, patterning sand.
                              And they
Were pale thin people, not often clear of town:
Elastic snapped, when he jerked off her hat:
I heard her arguing, 'Dick, my frock!' But he
Thought she was bread.
                    I wished her legs were brown,
And mostly, then, stared at the dawdling sea,
Hoping Perry would row me some day in his boat.

Not all the time; and when they'd gone, I went
Down to the hollow place where they had been,
Trickling bed through fingers. But I never meant
To tell the rest, or you, what I had seen:
Though that night, when I came in late for tea,
I hoped you'd see the sandgrains on my coat.

ROBIN HYDE

Bob Harvey

MAYOR, WAITAKERE CITY

Dear Cleo,

The Karekare Surf Club on Auckland's west coast has always been a long journey for club members. In 1935 when the club was founded they purchased an old bus which they left on the parking green while they all went off to war — needless to say it rusted away. We still find remnants of the vehicle after a flood.

On their return in 1947 they purchased an old army truck to take members from Auckland City to Karekare for patrol duties. On the dusty metal road out to the coast and then down the steep incline known as 'the cutting' it was always a hair-raising experience. I drove the truck myself for many years; often the brakes would fail and there would be accidents and skidding on the sharp corners. We all survived: the truck didn't — I lost it in a flood in the creek.

The poet Sam Sampson, whose great-uncles were founding members of the Karekare Surf Club and whose grandfather repaired the club truck, captures an earlier period with this poem. It thrills me with its excitement and evokes many memories of those hair-raising journeys out to the beach in my youth. The road is tar-sealed now but I still have fond memories of those days.

Best wishes,

R.A. Harvey

The Cutting

for George (Sam) Sampson

Changing down. Gravel separating;
middle ridge sprayed from tyre.
Pumping brakes until high on fluid.
Smoking drums exhausted. Light
shafts breaking kauri and teatree.
Blind corners . . . a leap of faith . . .
swinging wheels caught in corrugations.

Springs resisting pitted folds . . . Velocity
brushing arched toetoe . . .
                                        Foot pulsing.
Wheel arch nudging clay bank.

Boys on back, white knuckled grip
(holding on for dear life). Bumper
buffeting flax outcrops, slowing . . . stationary.

Boys leaping from tray.   *Alive!*

SAM SAMPSON

Carol Hirschfeld

EXECUTIVE PRODUCER, *CAMPBELL LIVE*

Dear Geraldine,

Firstly I am thrilled to be asked to contribute to the publication *Dear to Me*. To be asked to participate by my god-daughter made the request even more significant for me.

Here's my contribution:

The Search

Blown apart by loss, she let herself go —
wandered the neighborhood hatless, breasts
swinging under a ratty sweater, crusted
mascara blackening her gaze. It was a shame,
the wives whispered, to carry on so.
To them, wearing foam curlers arraigned
like piglets to market was almost debonair,
but an uncombed head? — not to be trusted.

The men watched more closely, tantalized
by so much indifference. Winter came early and still
she frequented the path by the river until
one with murmurous eyes pulled her down to size.
Sniffed Mrs. Franklin, ruling matron, to the rest:
Serves her right, the old mare.

RITA DOVE

This poem comes from a collection called *Mother Love* by Rita Dove. The collection, a series of sonnets, deals with the Greek myth of Demeter and Persephone. The form and subject may be classical but the setting is contemporary and suburban. I love the fact that Dove has chosen a poetic form that is restrictive yet so elegant in her hands. This particular poem does a beautiful job in evoking the suspicion and heat that raw grief can unwittingly reveal.

Best regards,

Carol Hirschfeld

Sam Hunt

POET

Dear Lisa,

Got your letter, thanks.

Choose a single poem?

There's an awful lot of stars, each in their own constellation, in the night sky of poetry.

Constellations with names like Yeats, James K. Baxter, Octavio Paz, Alistair Te Ariki Campbell, both Dylans, Robin Hyde, Leonard Cohen, Sylvia Plath . . . and on.

Choose one!

Okay. Right now I'm gazing at that sky, and all those stars.

Here's one. It's a star called 'Para Todos', in the constellation of Pablo Neruda. In English, 'For Everyone'.

Here's to you.

Sam Hunt

For Everyone

I can't just suddenly tell you
what I should be telling you,
friend, forgive me; you know
that although you don't hear my words,
I wasn't asleep or in tears,
that I'm with you without seeing you
for a good long time and until the end.

I know that many may wonder
'What is Pablo doing?' I'm here.
If you look for me in this street
you'll find me with my violin,
prepared to break into song,
prepared to die.

It is nothing I have to leave to anyone,
not to these others, not to you,
and if you listen well, in the rain,
you'll hear
that I come and go and hang about.
And you know that I have to leave.

Even if my words don't know it,
be sure, I'm the one who left.
There is no silence which doesn't end.
When the moment comes, expect me
and let them all know I'm arriving
in the street, with my violin.

PABLO NERUDA

Kevin Ireland

WRITER, POET

The Lover Showeth How He Is Forsaken
of Such as He Sometime Enjoyed

They flee from me, that sometime did me seek,
With naked foot stalking within my chamber:
Once have I seen them gentle, tame, and meek,
That now are wild, and do not once remember,
That sometime they have put themselves in danger
To take bread at my hand; and now they range
Busily seeking in continual change.

Thanked be fortune, it hath been otherwise
Twenty times better: but once especial,
In thin array, after a pleasant guise,
When her loose gown did from her shoulders fall,
And she me caught in her arms long and small,
And therewithal so sweetly did me kiss,
And softly said, 'Dear heart, how like you this?'

It was no dream; for I lay broad awaking:
But all is turn'd now through my gentleness,
Into a bitter fashion of forsaking;
And I have leave to go of her goodness;
And she also to use newfangleness.
But since that I unkindly so am served:
How like you this, what hath she now deserved?

SIR THOMAS WYATT

Dear Cleo,

I won't go into the textual problems of the several versions
of this poem, except to say that its first line frequently appears
as its title, which is sometimes spelt 'They fle from me that
sometyme did me seke'. For all its variations, the poem is
written in language that is close to modern English, and its
message, style and stance are stunningly fresh, although it
was written almost five centuries ago.

Wyatt served Henry VIII as a courtier and ambassador, and
was imprisoned twice in the Tower of London. He and Henry
Howard, Earl of Surrey, are often described as the fathers of the
English sonnet, though Wyatt, especially, experimented with
several other forms.

This poem was shrewdly described by James K. Baxter as one
of the few 'bedroom lyrics' in our language, but I feel that there
is more to it than that. One of the many things I love about it is
the way its lines bristle with energy and technical tricks, yet the
whole piece maintains perfect structural balance, even though
it seems possible that Wyatt may have set out to write a sonnet
(there are 14 lines in the first two stanzas, although the rhyme
scheme does not strictly follow the 'Italian' rules or Surrey's
'English' modifications), then it is almost as though the subject
matter overwhelmed him and he had to extend the form by half
again. It is worth noting how the first two lines of the poem
slip subtly from the plural to the singular and from the general
to the particular, preparing us for the storm of contrasts that
follow: it compares the past with the present, pleasure with
regret, tenderness with rage, giving with receiving, insinuation
with desertion, and a domestic and intimate physicality with
a vague sense of existing in perilous times – the poet has not
simply been abandoned, his lover has joined those who find it
expedient to 'flee' from him and he sprinkles about words such

as 'wild', 'danger', 'bitter' and 'forsaking'. The poem speaks to us from a far land and a distant era, but its accent remains forever contemporary. It is as sharp and new as the day it was penned.

Kevin Ireland

Sir Robert Jones

ENTREPRENEUR

Dear Cleo,

Thank you for your letter.

I'm afraid no poetry is actually dear to me; rather it's a blank and forms no part of my reading.

Having said that I will contribute as one poem has stuck with me from my school days to the extent that I quoted it last year in my last book, it being pertinent to the chapter's theme.

That is Shelley's 'Ozymandias'.

The reason why I like it is that it sums up so well the misplaced grandiose egotism of rulers, be they elected prime ministers or tyrants, and their craving for permanent legacy after their inevitable demise. It is an illogical aspiration: once dead, however they're viewed is utterly irrelevant to them as they'll never know. That reality doesn't stop retired prime ministers wasting their remaining years writing memoirs which they hope will preserve their place and perceived importance in history.

'Ozymandias' demonstrates the futility of such aspirations and the inevitable denouement for us all of reduction to dust.

Best wishes,

Sir Robert Jones

Ozymandias

I met a traveller from an antique land
Who said: Two vast and trunkless legs of stone
Stand in the desert. Near them on the sand,
Half sunk, a shatter'd visage lies, whose frown
And wrinkled lip and sneer of cold command
Tell that its sculptor well those passions read
Which yet survive, stamp'd on these lifeless things,
The hand that mock'd them and the heart that fed;
And on the pedestal these words appear:
'My name is Ozymandias, king of kings:
Look on my works, ye Mighty, and despair!'
Nothing beside remains. Round the decay
Of that colossal wreck, boundless and bare,
The lone and level sands stretch far away.

PERCY BYSSHE SHELLEY

Jane Kelsey

PROFESSOR OF LAW, UNIVERSITY OF AUCKLAND

Dear Shika,

Cecil Rajendra is a Malaysian poet and lawyer whom I met in the early 1980s when we were working on human rights violations in South East Asia. That was the era of dictatorships in Singapore under Lee Kwan Yew, Malaysia under Mahathir Mohammed, Philippines under Ferdinand Marcos, Indonesia under Suharto and too many more. By his remarkable blend of lawyer and poet Cecil was able to bring his passion for human rights and justice into both worlds.

Cecil's book of poetry entitled *Hour of Assassins and Other Poems* was dedicated to 'Walter Rodney – historian, scholar, activist and brother', an inspirational leader who was persecuted in his native Guyana and assassinated in a bomb explosion in 1980 while running for office in the national elections.

This particular poem, 'The Dark Side of Trees', serves as an enduring reminder of our responsibilities as lawyers and public voices, and simply as human beings. It is as poignant in 2006 – as the world turns its back on fundamental principles of justice and human rights, and people retreat into silence – as it was when I first read it in 1984.

Good luck with the project.

Warm regards,

Jane Kelsey

The Dark Side of Trees

The truth burns
so they turned
their faces away
from the sun . . .

When small liberties
            began to fray . . .
When their constitution
            was being chipped away
When their newspapers
            were shut down . . .
When their rule of law
            was twisted round . . .
When might became right
            and their friends
Were carried off screaming
            in the pitch of night . . .

They chose silence
feigned blindness
pleaded ignorance.

And now when the shadow
            of the jackboot hangs
ominous over their beloved land
            they walk as zombies
unable to distinguish right from
            wrong from right
their minds furred with lichens
            like the dark side of trees.

The truth burns
so they turned
their faces away
from the sun . . .

CECIL RAJENDRA

Dame Fiona Kidman

NOVELIST, POET

Dear Va,

The poet Lauris Edmond was one of my closest friends for some 28 years. She lived round the corner in Grass Street in Wellington, a short walk from my house. I was a frequent visitor up until the time of her sudden death in early 2000. We shared similar views of the city's sea and sky, only her outlook included gum trees which remind me very much of my own childhood up north. She captures, in a simple straightforward way, both the exact feeling of this beautiful environment, and the shapes of the trees, in a way that acts as metaphor for a person growing old. In spite of the sense of her own mortality running beneath the lines of 'At Grass Street', she celebrates the exhilaration of the moment and her belief that life should be lived to the full. The lovely line 'we leave best what we have truly loved' speaks directly to me of her generous approach to life.

Fiona Kidman

At Grass Street

It is spring, a cool windy evening,
the gum trees are turning, leaves grey
and grained where they curve out
from the spine, grey too the moving sea water;
clouds are constantly changing position

and the hill falling away so fast it seems
to move too with an urgent clambering gait,
shifting and sifting, one grain on another in
a perpetual unwillingness to settle for
what the world is at one moment of its turning;

while my body, apparently still, follows
each cell of earth, air, in a moving emulsion,
ordered exhilaration so fierce
it can only be quelled by this setting it down —
for you who later will stand here, and of course

not care at all, having your own weather
and trees, hills falling and finding their
eternally temporary poise . . . all the same,
we leave best what we have truly loved, and now
I turn easily away, one second nearer my death.

LAURIS EDMOND

Cindy Kiro

CHILDREN'S COMMISSIONER

Libby,

Here is an excerpt from Shakespeare (not really a poem, I know, but recited as one to me as a child). It is from Portia's speech in *The Merchant of Venice*.

> The quality of mercy is not strain'd,
> It droppeth as the gentle rain from heaven
> Upon the place beneath: it is twice blest;
> It blesseth him that gives, and him that takes;
> 'Tis mightiest in the mightiest: it becomes
> The throned monarch better than his crown;
> His sceptre shows the force of temporal power,
> The attribute to awe and majesty,
> Wherein doth sit the dread and fear of kings;
> But mercy is above this sceptred sway;
> It is enthroned in the hearts of kings,
> It is an attribute to God himself;
> And earthly power doth then show likest God's
> When mercy seasons justice.

This was oft quoted to me as a child by my godfather, for whom this was a favourite. I learned to associate with him the intonation and words and the fun times we had, and also learned the meaning of the ideas behind the words and their power, as I grew up. He has died now, but the power of the poem lives on.

This poem or speech is about justice and mercy, and the importance of these over other temporal and material things in the world. It is these qualities that we should most value. It puts us beyond temporary concerns.

Justice is a concept I have spent most of my life committed to in some way or other — trying to make sure that those who are least able to speak for themselves have someone who is prepared to speak for them or with them.

Mercy is at the heart of justice. It is the quintessential human characteristic that lifts us above ourselves and makes us capable, ultimately, of behaving compassionately, humanely and respectfully. These are the values that matter most to me.

Cindy Kiro

Chris Knox

MUSICIAN, SONGWRITER

Dear Va,

I'm no poetry lover, can't be bothered trying to work out what the poet's trying to say or why they end their lines in such strange places, but I can't resist a good song lyric. Even if I'm not entirely sure what it may mean. Which is the case with my choice here, Dave Yetton's 'Flex' – as recorded by Christchurch's Jean Paul Sartre Experience on their debut Flying Nun 12" EP in 1986.

It's always been my favourite Kiwi chorus, rare in this country for actually being about lovemaking – or, at the very least, sex – and talking about it in less than glowing terms. 'But it's not' is devastating in this context. A terrifying glimpse of the alone-ness that we all share. I also feel that the line: 'Well I don't know the physics of the affair/or if I'm even needed' is as close to verbal genius as I've heard come off a slab of vinyl. It says so much about male angst and doubt and references the radical feminist/lesbian/artificial insemination era in which it was written with concise, effortless accuracy.

The first and last verses are more obscure . . . but make sense on a purely aural level – like all great verse built to be accompanied by music.

Now go search it out on CD – and get the full picture.

Cheers,

Chris

Flex

A monastic life built on postcards bright
and lots of friends to share it,
well, you've got a lot to say for yourself
but I don't really want to hear it.

Flex thyself, and muscle me in
like we're in this together
and it's a comforting thing . . . but it's not.

Well I don't know the physics of the affair
or if I'm even needed,
but I can't blame her for looming that way
you always go for what you're wanting.

Flex thyself, and muscle me in
like we're in this together
and it's a comforting thing . . . but it's not.

You rip off her skin and turn and tell me
she is ugly beneath it,
well that's funny 'cos I thought you were friends
but you really mean it.

Flex thyself, and muscle me in
like we're in this together
and it's a comforting thing . . . but it's not.

DAVE YETTON

Luamanuvao Winnie Laban

MINISTER FOR THE COMMUNITY AND VOLUNTARY SECTOR

Dear Esther,

Thank you for the invitation to participate in the *Dear to Me* project that the Auckland Girls' Grammar School Amnesty International Group is producing.

My favourite poem is 'Parents & Children' by Albert Wendt. It speaks to me of family, of history, of identity, of continuity, of culture, and of my place of belonging. I love Albert Wendt's profound words: 'Our Dead are the splendid robes our souls wear.'

Warm Pacific Greetings,

Hon Luamanuvao Winnie Laban

Parents & Children

Parents and their children come
to one another through many doors
that laugh, slap, clap, slash, bleed
block, cry, and let-you-through sometimes.
And by the time they meet
they've been sieved to the rags and bones
of who they were and can't remember.

Around our house mynah birds
dart and dive. I count
the holes they pierce in the sky.
My son is in the garage fixing
the brakes of his bike.
In her bedroom my daughter
is locked into Captain America.

I've left believing in God,
my children are starting towards Him.
I carry willingly the heritage of my Dead,
my children have yet to recognise theirs.
Someday before they leave our house
forever I'll tell them: 'Our Dead
are the splendid robes our souls wear.'

The armada of mynah birds continues
to attack the trees and sky.
Their ferocity cuts wounds
in my thoughts.
Through those wounds like doors
I'll go this morning
to meet my children.

ALBERT WENDT

Keith Locke

MEMBER OF PARLIAMENT

Dear Geraldine,

I have chosen 'No Ordinary Sun' by the New Zealand poet
Hone Tuwhare, and published in his first book, entitled
No Ordinary Sun.

No Ordinary Sun

Tree let your arms fall:
raise them not sharply in supplication
to the bright enhaloed cloud.
Let your arms lack toughness and
resilience for this is no mere axe
to blunt nor fire to smother.

Your sap shall not rise again
to the moon's pull.
No more incline a deferential head
to the wind's talk, or stir
to the tickle of coursing rain.

Your former shagginess shall not be
wreathed with the delightful flight
of birds nor shield
nor cool the ardour of unheeding
lovers from the monstrous sun.

Tree let your naked arms fall
nor extend vain entreaties to the radiant ball.

This is no gallant monsoon's flash,
no dashing trade wind's blast.
The fading green of your magic
emanations shall not make pure again
these polluted skies . . . for this
is no ordinary sun.

O tree
in the shadowless mountains
the white plains and
the drab sea floor
your end at last is written.

HONE TUWHARE

'No Ordinary Sun' made a deep impression on me when it came out in 1964. As a young student I had been on Hiroshima Day marches, and through the Cuban missile crisis, and I was very worried about the danger of nuclear war. I was also a keen tramper and loved the New Zealand bush.

The poem vividly portrayed the nuclear apocalypse where life itself would disappear. The medium of trees worked for me because they were so much part of my being – and the poem connected them so seamlessly with the rest of nature, and with people.

I have always thought that the title 'No Ordinary Sun', three simple words, has such power. Kiwi 'understatement' can be very effective.

Regards,

Keith Locke

Andy Lovelock

DETECTIVE SUPERINTENDENT, NEW ZEALAND POLICE

Dear Va,

After reading this poem you can tell that John Masefield was not the English Poet Laureate for nothing!

In three short verses he has managed to capture a sense of urgency, passion, romance, adventure and daring that I have found to be truly inspirational over many years.

As you read, you can actually *see* the wind in the sails; and feel the sea-spray burning your face, as goose bumps rise on the back of your neck.

As a would-be 'vagrant gypsy', I love the sea, the sky and the wild — and for more than a quarter of a century I have escaped to the wilderness and tranquillity of Coromandel's west coast beaches whenever I can.

On a deeper plain, 'Sea-Fever' is really a reflection of our lives — and what they can mean, and be.

The 'lonely sea and the sky' is an image of life itself as it stretches out before us.

Aboard a 'tall ship' signifies our journey through it.

A 'star to steer her by' speaks of the life-values or the morality that we hold dear to guide our passage.

And, 'all I ask is a merry yarn from a laughing fellow-rover' expresses our desire for 'kin-ship' and a sense of belonging with like-minded travellers.

A 'quiet sleep and a sweet dream when the long trick's over' motivates and encourages us to strive for an achieving, fulfilled life – where at the end we can claim, with our heads held high, that we have run the good race without any sense of remorse, before fading away in contentment when the enigma of life comes to a close.

Boy, that's some poem – outstanding!

Andy Lovelock

Sea-Fever

I must down to the seas again, to the lonely sea and the sky,
And all I ask is a tall ship and a star to steer her by,
And the wheel's kick and the wind's song and the white
    sail's shaking,
And a grey mist on the sea's face, and a grey dawn breaking.

I must down to the seas again, for the call of the running tide
Is a wild call and a clear call that may not be denied;
And all I ask is a windy day with the white clouds flying,
And the flung spray and the blown spume, and the sea-gulls
    crying.

I must down to the seas again, to the vagrant gypsy life,
To the gull's way and the whale's way where the wind's like a
    whetted knife;
And all I ask is a merry yarn from a laughing fellow-rover
And quiet sleep and a sweet dream when the long trick's over.

JOHN MASEFIELD

Dave McArtney

MUSICIAN

Dear Libby,

Sorry, I have to walk through this poem, right now, because its beauty lies in its process and unpoetic (is there such a word?) simplicity.

A seemingly aimless meander, almost childlike, kind of contrary, of dislocated trivia, of a man killing time in a New York street. There is a hint of superficiality and shallow literary pretensions; a monologue of mundane plans, the purchase of perfunctory gifts for his dinner hosts later that evening, and an unsettling anxiety and loneliness at the thought of having to travel out of his comfort zone to this social occasion. It all sounds so normal, so self-obsessed.

Through a panoply of NYC icons, land-marked and namedropped, to almost 'going to sleep with quandariness' in a bookshop as he tries to decide on the book gift, amidst the distraction of his own browsing through an odd juxtaposition of classics, an Irish playwright, and gay French literature.

So, we are delivered to a reverent tribute to Billie Holiday – the numbness of death, and the voided reaction to its news, here, the death of a great, but tragically flawed blues singer – framed by O'Hara's recollection of the singer in a subdued, opiated state, in a 'whispered' performance in the bowels of a sleazy jazz club.

Powerful in its understatement! We sympathise with the emotional paucity of the poet, as it's deftly and truthfully portrayed. It is also a universal theme. We all have had that same stark experience of what you were doing and where you were when the news of the sudden death of a famous person, in shockingly tragic circumstances, came to hand. Where were you when John Lennon died? Yes, indeed.

I revisit this poem often because it takes me back to that feeling of being immersed in New York City for the first time – the streets, the beat culture, that sexy Manhattan nonchalance, the exhaustion! But, with this poem, you cannot ignore its completeness. Its skilful control on a number of levels, to the ultimate conclusion that we all become at one with Miss Holiday when 'everyone and I stopped breathing'. A moment of magnificent coherence, for the poem!

It is a statement of time and mortality as well as a statement of the state of modern poetry – in 1959! – or a statement of the essential importance of poetry to modern life, to reinstall feeling, where feeling has been stolen away by modern life.

I love this unassuming little piece of writing, though certainly not one of my *favourite* poems – one could have gone for the joy of a Yeats, or the mysterious grace of a Shakespeare sonnet – however, perhaps something grey and narcotic which struggles with inertia befits the urgency and importance of Amnesty International.

Dave McArtney

The Day Lady Died

It is 12:20 in New York a Friday
three days after Bastille day, yes
it is 1959 and I go get a shoeshine
because I will get off the 4:19 in Easthampton
at 7:15 and then go straight to dinner
and I don't know the people who will feed me

I walk up the muggy street beginning to sun
and have a hamburger and a malted and buy
an ugly NEW WORLD WRITING to see what the poets
in Ghana are doing these days
                                    I go on to the bank
and Miss Stillwagon (first name Linda I once heard)
doesn't even look up my balance for once in her life
and in the GOLDEN GRIFFIN I get a little Verlaine
for Patsy with drawings by Bonnard although I do
think of Hesiod, trans. Richmond Lattimore or
Brendan Behan's new play or *Le Balcon* or *Le Nègres*
of Genet, but I don't, I stick with Verlaine
after practically going to sleep with quandariness

and for Mike I just stroll into the PARK LANE
Liquor Store and ask for a bottle of Strega and
then I go back where I came from to 6th Avenue
and the tobacconist in the Ziegfeld Theatre and a carton
of Picayunes, and a NEW YORK POST with her face on it

and I am sweating a lot by now and thinking of
leaning on the john door in the 5 SPOT
while she whispered along the keyboard
to Mal Waldron and everyone and I stopped breathing

FRANK O'HARA

Finlay Macdonald

JOURNALIST, EDITOR

Hi Geraldine,

The poem I've chosen is 'Children' by Bill Manhire.

Why did I choose it? Well, being asked to pick a favourite poem is like being asked to choose a favourite child. It's impossible. But thinking that did remind me of this one and why I like it so much. It's not a complicated or particularly difficult poem, but it speaks beautifully about the bitter-sweet joys of being a parent, and being mortal. I've always enjoyed art of any kind that plays with the idea of time and its passage, and which makes you look at life in surprising ways. This is about letting go and not letting go of the things we love, a moving little poem that rings true to me.

All the best,

Finlay Macdonald

Children

The likelihood is
the children will die
without you to help them do it.
It will be spring,
the light on the water,
or not.

And though at present
they live together
they will not die together.
They will die one by one
and not think to call you:
they will be old

and you will be gone.
It will be spring,
or not. They may be crossing
the road,
not looking left,
not looking right,

or may simply be afloat at evening
like clouds unable
to make repairs. That
one talks too much, that one
hardly at all: and they both enjoy
the light on the water

much as we enjoy
the sense
of indefinite postponement. Yes
it's a tall story but don't you think
full of promise, and he's just a kid
but watch him grow.

BILL MANHIRE

Don McGlashan

MUSICIAN

Dear Va,

One of my favourite poems is 'Inversnaid' by Gerard Manley
Hopkins. I stumbled on it in Ted Hughes's anthology *By Heart*
when I was touring a lot around Europe with the band. We
must have accidentally bought the special Depressives' Edition
of the *A to Z*, because the autobahns we took all seemed to be
painted hospital grey, and whenever the countryside threatened
to get interesting, it was quickly hidden behind tall grey sound-
barriers. In the back of the van on long trips, I often used to
recite this one over and over to myself, partly because of the
way it sounds – the poet's wholehearted love of words for their
own sake – and partly because of the way it seems to tumble
recklessly along like the stream it describes, reminding me of all
the anarchic, wild nature back home.

Don

Inversnaid

This darksome burn, horseback brown,
His rollrock highroad roaring down,
In coop and in comb the fleece of his foam
Flutes and low to the lake falls home.

A windpuff-bonnet of fawn-froth
Turns and twindles over the broth
Of a pool so pitchblack, fell-frowning,
It rounds and rounds Despair to drowning.

Degged with dew, dappled with dew
Are the groins of the braes that the brook treads through,
Wiry heathpacks, flitches of fern,
And the beadbonny ash that sits over the burn.

What would the world be, once bereft
Of wet and wildness? Let them be left,
O let them be left, wildness and wet;
Long live the weeds and the wilderness yet.

GERARD MANLEY HOPKINS

Elizabeth McRae

ACTOR

Dear Esther,

Thank you so much for your letter. I'm very pleased to be part
of this project as I'm a poetry lover and an Amnesty supporter.
The poem I have chosen is by Fleur Adcock. I think I originally
snipped it out of the *Listener*. I now find that it was published
in 1986 by Oxford University Press in a collection of Fleur
Adcock's poems called *The Incident Book*.

The title of the poem is 'The Chiffonier'. What a lovely word
for a dresser.

The poem really speaks to me — maybe because I have two
daughters and four granddaughters and the mother is possibly
about my age. New Zealand families are often flung wide
around the world. Hearts are tugged with 'Home Thoughts from
Abroad'. Daughters and mothers seek each other out and try to
say what they mean to each other.

The form of this poem is conversational and the tone is wistful
and poignant.

Sincerely,

Elizabeth McRae

The Chiffonier

You're glad I like the chiffonier. But I
feel suddenly uneasy, scenting why
you're pleased I like this pretty thing you've bought,
the twin of one that stood beside your cot
when you were small: you've marked it down for me;
it's not too heavy to be sent by sea
when the time comes, and it's got space inside
to pack some other things you've set aside,
things that are small enough to go by water
twelve thousand miles to me, your English daughter.
I know your habits – writing all our names
in books and on the backs of picture-frames,
allotting antique glass and porcelain dishes
to granddaughters according to their wishes,
promising me the tinted photograph
of my great-grandmother. We used to laugh,
seeing how each occasional acquisition
was less for you than for later disposition:
'You know how Marilyn likes blue and white
china? I've seen some plates I thought I might
indulge in.' Bless you, Mother! But we're not
quite so inclined to laugh now that you've got
something that's new to you but not a part
of your estate: that weakness in your heart.
It makes my distance from you, when I go
back home next week, suddenly swell and grow
from thirty hours' flying to a vast
galactic space between present and past.
How many more times can I hope to come
to Wellington and find you still at home?
We've talked about it, as one has to, trying
to see the lighter aspects of your dying:

'You've got another twenty years or more'
I said, 'but when you think you're at death's door
just let me know. I'll come and hang about
for however long it takes to see you out.'
'I don't think it'll be like that' you said:
'I'll pop off suddenly one night in bed.'
How secretive! How satisfying! You'll
sneak off, a kid running away from school —
well, that at least's the only way I find
I can bring myself to see it in my mind.
But now I see you in your Indian skirt
and casual cornflower-blue linen shirt
in the garden, under your feijoa tree,
looking about as old or young as me.
Dear little Mother! Naturally I'm glad
you found a piece of furniture that had
happy associations with your youth;
and yes, I do admire it — that's the truth:
its polished wood and touch of Art Nouveau
appeal to me. But surely you must know
I value this or any other treasure
of yours chiefly because it gives you pleasure.
I have to write this now, while you're still here:
I want my mother, not her chiffonier.

FLEUR ADCOCK

Margaret Mahy

CHILDREN'S AUTHOR, WINNER OF THE CARNEGIE
AND HANS CHRISTIAN ANDERSEN MEDALS

Hello Libby,

I am sorry to have been so long in sending you a poem. Of course part of the trouble is that one has so many favourites that one puts off making a decision. Anyhow I thought I would send one of my shorter favourites . . . one that is rather obscure, so it may not be duplicating any other favourite. (I imagine you might have quite a number of Shakespeare sonnets submitted.)

A blast of wind, a momentary breath,
A watery bubble symboliz'd with air,
A sun-blown rose, but for a season fair,
A ghostly glance, a skeleton of death:
A morning dew, pearling the grass beneath,
Whose moisture sun's appearance doth impair;
A lightning glimpse, a muse of thought and care,
A planet's shot, a shade which followeth,
A voice which vanisheth so soon as heard,
The thriftless heir of time, a rolling wave,
A show, no more in action than regard,
A mass of dust, world's momentary slave,
        Is man, in state of our old Adam made,
        Soon born to die, soon flourishing to fade.

BARNABE BARNES

And here is a poem I loved as a child . . .

Who said, 'Peacock Pie'?
   The old King to the sparrow:
Who said, 'Crops are ripe'?
   Rust to the harrow:
Who said, 'Where sleeps she now?
   Where rests she now her head,
Bathed in eve's loveliness'? −
   That's what I said.

Who said, 'Ay, mum's the word'?
   Sexton to willow:
Who said 'Green dusk for dreams,
   Moss for a pillow'?
Who said, 'All Time's delight
   Hath she for narrow bed;
Life's troubled bubble broken'? −
   That's what I said.

WALTER DE LA MARE

I hope these short poems fit into your collection. I mean there are great poems like 'The Love Song of J. Alfred Prufrock' and so on, but I imagine you might welcome short poems that might fit easily into half a page.

Best wishes,

Margaret Mahy

Owen Marshall

WRITER

Dear Shika,

I would prefer that my favourite poem was not as
conventionally popular as this, and almost everything I have
read about Dylan Thomas suggests a personality I would dislike,
nevertheless I cannot deny the power I find in this poem. That
emotional power, and the theme which it drives, are almost
entire within the first three-line stanza. And what a stroke of
genius to use the adjective, gentle, rather than the expected
adverb.

Regards,

Owen Marshall

Do Not Go Gentle into that Good Night

Do not go gentle into that good night,
Old age should burn and rave at close of day;
Rage, rage against the dying of the light.

Though wise men at their end know dark is right,
Because their words had forked no lightning they
Do not go gentle into that good night.

Good men, the last wave by, crying how bright
Their frail deeds might have danced in a green bay,
Rage, rage against the dying of the light.

Wild men who caught and sang the sun in flight,
And learn, too late, they grieved it on its way,
Do not go gentle into that good night.

Grave men, near death, who see with blinding sight
Blind eyes could blaze like meteors and be gay,
Rage, rage against the dying of the light.

And you, my father, there on the sad height,
Curse, bless, me now with your fierce tears, I pray.
Do not go gentle into that good night.
Rage, rage against the dying of the light.

DYLAN THOMAS

Lesley Max

CHILD ADVOCATE – CEO OF GREAT POTENTIALS, WHICH OPERATES
HIPPY AND MATES PROGRAMMES

Dear Va,

Thank you for inviting me to participate in this project, which really touched me personally. My mother, Flora Shieff (nee Shenkin) who taught speech and drama at AGGS, was much loved by a generation of women – her former pupils – many of whom learned to love poetry through her, as I did.

This poem, W.B. Yeats's 'Lake Isle of Innisfree', was one we both loved. I recorded her reading it when she was 91 years old, with the beautiful timbre of her voice evoking the tranquillity Yeats was yearning for and which so appeals to me. She was able to make the poet's words and rhythms paint pictures, create moods and open 'magic casements' on to Innisfree, far away.

I think it brought her memories of her happiness as a child, living with her family on the shores of Lake Pupuke, before the First World War.

With best wishes for your book,

Lesley Max

The Lake Isle of Innisfree

I will arise and go now, and go to Innisfree,
And a small cabin build there, of clay and wattles made:
Nine bean-rows will I have there, a hive for the honey-bee,
And live alone in the bee-loud glade.

And I shall have some peace there, for peace comes
    dropping slow,
Dropping from the veils of the morning to where the
    cricket sings;
There midnight's all a glimmer, and noon a purple glow,
And evening full of the linnet's wings.

I will arise and go now, for always night and day
I hear lake water lapping with low sounds by the shore;
While I stand on the roadway, or on the pavements grey,
I hear it in the deep heart's core.

W.B. YEATS

Bernice Mene

FORMER SILVER FERN CAPTAIN

Dear Libby,

I hunted through my poetry books in the bookshelf and nothing jumped out at me — then I found a book of my own scribbles and this one made me smile as it is a short 'ditty' longing for my childhood days of bright lavalava holidays, a bed full of soft toys, Mum reading to my brothers and me at night, and the jellybean jar at the doctor's!

Cheers,

Bernie

Child at Heart

The king has lost his crown
And I my childhood friends
The jellybean jar's gone down
Though still far from the end

Surround yourself with stories
The ones that last a while
Drown yourself in colour
Bright hues to make me smile

I can taste Charlie's chocolate
Hear Pooh hum tiddley poms
Take me through the looking glass
Back where I belong

BERNICE MENE

Jim Moriarty

ACTOR, DIRECTOR

Kia ora Cleo,

Thanks for the opportunity to participate in the *Dear to Me* project.

I have chosen W.H. Auden's poem 'Refugee Blues' because it was as an adolescent that I first came across it whilst a student at St Patrick's College in Wellington.

The overriding educational thrust at that time, and as now, inside that particular system was to produce young men and women, who developed a sincere sense of empathy/compassion for their fellow human beings. Auden's poem stands today as it did then, not only as a testament to the holocaust journey but also as an enduring reminder and metaphor to all people who fight against extreme expressions in their battle for survival as individuals, cultures and nations.

Noho ora mai,

Jim Moriarty

Refugee Blues

Say this city has ten million souls,
Some are living in mansions, some are living in holes:
Yet there's no place for us, my dear, yet there's no place
    for us.

Once we had a country and we thought it fair,
Look in the atlas and you'll find it there:
We cannot go there now, my dear, we cannot go there
now.

In the village churchyard there grows an old yew,
Every spring it blossoms anew:
Old passports can't do that, my dear, old passports can't
    do that.

The consul banged the table and said,
'If you've got no passport you're officially dead':
But we are still alive, my dear, but we are still alive.

Went to a committee; they offered me a chair;
Asked me politely to return next year:
But where shall we go to-day, my dear, but where shall
    we go to-day?

Came to a public meeting; the speaker got up and said;
'If we let them in, they will steal our daily bread':
He was talking of you and me, my dear, he was talking of
    you and me.

Thought I heard the thunder rumbling in the sky;
It was Hitler over Europe, saying, 'They must die':
O we were in his mind, my dear, O we were in his mind.

Saw a poodle in a jacket fastened with a pin,
Saw a door opened and a cat let in:
But they weren't German Jews, my dear, but they weren't
German Jews.

Went down the harbour and stood upon the quay,
Saw the fish swimming as if they were free:
Only ten feet away, my dear, only ten feet away.

Walked through a wood, saw the birds in the trees;
They had no politicians and sang at their ease:
They weren't the human race, my dear, they weren't the
human race.

Dreamed I saw a building with a thousand floors,
A thousand windows and a thousand doors:
Not one of them was ours, my dear, not one of them was
ours.

Stood on a great plain in the falling snow;
Ten thousand soldiers marched to and fro:
Looking for you and me, my dear, looking for you and me.

W.H. AUDEN

Graham Mourie

FORMER ALL BLACK CAPTAIN

Hi Libby,

Moana our daughter loves her poetry and this is one her teacher sent home a couple of years ago. She has moved on a bit since then but still likes this one. So do we – inspired by the Wellington climate.

Kind regards,

Graham Mourie

The Storm

The rain splashed into colossal ponds
while the trees wailed
Go away my dear leaves, glide to somewhere sheltered
The wind smashing, smacking, slamming into anything in
its path – furious in rage
After the battle it's like a bombsite
The animals are hungry and cold
The ponds still as can be
Leaves peeking out of hiding places
The trees moaning and groaning in the cold background.

MOANA MOURIE (2004, AGED 7)

Rosslyn Noonan

CHIEF COMMISSIONER, HUMAN RIGHTS COMMISSION

Dear Geraldine,

I am delighted to be part of this project.

'Journey of the Magi' retells an old story vividly, graphically, evoking places and people as powerfully as any painting. Indeed in 50 years of reading novels, history, biographies and travel books I have never come across another account of a journey that has had such an impact. The voice of the Magi recalling this seminal experience is so strong that as I read the poem it is as if I am actually hearing his gravely, gruff, questioning, world weary, despairing tones. This poem requires no academic analysis to understand it. Yet, in addition to the immense pleasure of the language, its succinctness and sensuousness, each reading reveals something more. It is a poem that draws me into a 2000-year-old event and leaves me with something of the Magi's sense of unease, of dislocation. It provokes and challenges.

Warmest regards,

Rosslyn

Journey of the Magi

'A cold coming we had of it,
Just the worst time of the year
For a journey, and such a long journey:
The ways deep and the weather sharp,
The very dead of winter.'
And the camels galled, sore-footed, refractory,
Lying down in the melted snow.
There were times we regretted
The summer palaces on slopes, the terraces,
And the silken girls bringing sherbet.
Then the camel men cursing and grumbling
And running away, and wanting their liquor and women,
And the night-fires going out, and the lack of shelters,
And the cities hostile and the towns unfriendly
And the villages dirty and charging high prices:
A hard time we had of it.
At the end we preferred to travel all night,
Sleeping in snatches,
With the voices singing in our ears, saying
That this was all folly.

Then at dawn we came down to a temperate valley,
Wet, below the snow line, smelling of vegetation,
With a running stream and a water-mill beating the darkness,
And three trees on the low sky.
An old white horse galloped away in the meadow.
Then we came to a tavern with vine-leaves over the lintel,
Six hands at an open door dicing for pieces of silver,
And feet kicking the empty wine-skins.
But there was no information, and so we continued
And arrived at evening, not a moment too soon
Finding the place; it was (you may say) satisfactory.

All this was a long time ago, I remember,
And I would do it again, but set down
This set down
This: were we led all that way for
Birth or Death? There was a Birth, certainly,
We had evidence and no doubt. I had seen birth and death,
But had thought they were different; this Birth was
Hard and bitter agony for us, like Death, our death.
We returned to our places, these Kingdoms,
But no longer at ease here, in the old dispensation,
With an alien people clutching their gods.
I should be glad of another death.

T.S. ELIOT

Rod Oram

JOURNALIST

Libby, hello!

My choice is Denis Glover's 'Home Thoughts' . . . the 1981 short version. Apparently he wrote a longer version in 1936.

My family and I emigrated from England to New Zealand in 1997. We came because it seemed to us New Zealand was making its future while England was defending its past. Thus, we thought it would be far more fulfilling to live and work here rather than there. We were right . . . and the poem expresses that much more beautifully than we ever could.

I could have chosen Allen Curnow's 'Landfall in Unknown Seas' . . . for exploring the same idea about New Zealand's future but in very heroic terms (since it was written for the 300th anniversary of Tasman's landfall) such as

> Simply by sailing in a new direction
> You could enlarge the world.

And . . .

>   Who reaches
> A future down for us from the high shelf
> Of spiritual daring?

And because I'm a huge fan of Lilburn's music, his wonderful tone poems of this land. He set this Curnow poem to music in 1942. I have a 1994 recording of it played by the New Zealand Chamber Orchestra with Ed Hillary reading the poem.

All the very best with the project . . . and please let me know when I can buy a copy or two.

Rod

Home Thoughts

I do not dream of Sussex downs
or quaint old England's
quaint old towns –
I think of what may yet be seen
In Johnsonville or Geraldine.

DENIS GLOVER

Lance O'Sullivan

CHAMPION JOCKEY

Dear Lisa,

This is without doubt, one of the all-time greats. Any person who works with horses can relate to the bravery of this amazing animal.

Every Christmas Day in our household this poem is read by one of our family members. It is a bit of a tear-jerker.

Lance O'Sullivan ONZM

The Story of Mongrel Grey

This is the story the stockman told
   On the cattle camp, when the stars were bright;
The moon rose up like a globe of gold
    And flooded the plain with her mellow light.
        We watched the cattle till dawn of day
        And he told me the story of Mongrel Grey.

*   *   *

He was a knockabout station hack,
   Spurred and walloped, and banged and beat;
Ridden all day with a sore on his back,
    Left all night with nothing to eat.
        That was a matter of everyday
        Normal occurrence with Mongrel Grey.

We might have sold him, but someone heard
    He was bred Out Back on a flooded run,
Where he learnt to swim like a waterbird;
    Midnight or midday were all as one —
            In the flooded ground he would find his way;
            Nothing could puzzle old Mongrel Grey.

'Tis a trick, no doubt, that some horses learn;
    When the floods are out they will splash along
In girth-deep water, and twist and turn
    From hidden channel and billabong,
            Never mistaking the road to go;
            For a man may guess — but the horses *know*.

I was camping out with my youngest son —
    Bit of a nipper, just learnt to speak —
In an empty hut on the lower run,
    Shooting and fishing in Conroy's Creek.
            The youngster toddled about all day,
            And there with our horses was Mongrel Grey.

All of a sudden a flood came down,
    At first a freshet of mountain rain,
Roaring and eddying, rank and brown,
    Over the flats and across the plain.
            Rising and rising — at fall of night
            Nothing but water appeared in sight!

'Tis a nasty place when the floods are out,
    Even in daylight; for all around
Channels and billabongs twist about,
    Stretching for miles in the flooded ground.
            And to move seemed a hopeless thing to try
            In the dark with the storm-water racing by.

I had to risk it, I heard a roar
    As the wind swept down and the driving rain;
And the water rose till it reached the floor
    Of our highest room; and 'twas very plain –
        The way the torrent was sweeping down –
        We must make for the highlands at once, or drown.

Off to the stable I splashed, and found
    The horses shaking with cold and fright;
I led them down to the lower ground,
    But never a yard would they swim that night!
        They reared and snorted and turned away,
        And none would face it but Mongrel Grey.

I bound the child on the horse's back,
    And we started off, with a prayer to heaven,
Through the rain and the wind and the pitchy black,
    For I knew that the instinct God has given
        To prompt His creatures by night and day
        Would guide the footsteps of Mongrel Grey.

He struck deep water at once and swam –
    I swam beside him and held his mane –
Till we touched the bank of the broken dam
    In shallow water; then off again,
        Swimming in darkness across the flood,
        Rank with the smell of the drifting mud.

He turned and twisted across and back,
    Choosing the places to wade or swim,
Picking the safest and shortest track –
    The blackest darkness was clear to him.
        Did he strike the crossing by sight or smell?
        The Lord that led him alone could tell!

He dodged the timber whene'er he could,
  But timber brought us to grief at last;
I was partly stunned by a log of wood
  That struck my head as it drifted past;
      Then lost my grip of the brave old grey,
      And in half a second he swept away.

I reached a tree, where I had to stay,
  And did a perish for two days hard;
And lived on water – but Mongrel Grey,
  He walked right into the homestead yard
      At dawn next morning, and grazed around,
      With the child strapped on to him safe and sound.

We keep him now for the wife to ride,
  Nothing too good for him now, of course;
Never a whip on his fat old hide,
  For she owes the child to that brave grey horse.
      And not Old Tyson himself could pay
      The purchase money of Mongrel Grey.

ANDREW BARTON (BANJO) PATERSON

Merimeri Penfold

HUMAN RIGHTS COMMISSIONER

Kia ora Lisa,

I wrote the haka 'Kia Whakapakeha Au I Ahau' at the time the
New Zealand Rugby Union decided to play against South Africa
by permitting Maori players to be categorised as 'honorary whites'.

Kia Whakapākeha Au I Ahau

Ko te ao e ngunguru nei!
Au, au, aue hā!
Ko te ao e ngunguru nei!
Au, au, aue hā!
Kia whakapākeha au i ahau?
E kore, e kore, e kore, e!
Kia whakapākeha au i ahau?
E kore, e kore, e kore, e!
Upokokohua!
Taurekareka!
Upokokohua!
Taurekareka!
He tangata, he taniwha!
He tangata, he taniwha!
Au, au, aue ha!
Tū whakapakaka ki te ra!
Tū whakapakoko ki te ao!
Aue! Taukuri e!
He taniwha, he tipua!
He tipua, he taniwha!
He tipua, he tangata!
Tiheia Mauriora hei!

The world thunders and roars
Listen and behold
Hear the shot of defiance
And tumultuous challenge
Me, an honorary white?
Never, never, no never!
An honorary white?
Never, ever!
Curse you your cooked head!
Spawn of the devil!
Heap curses upon you!
Slave that you are!
Behold, a demon
A mighty demon
Exposed black by the sun
Carved grimace to the world
'tis a demon, a dinosaur
A dinosaur, a demon
Awesome sight
Behold! Remain staunch.

My second contribution is 'Elegy Written in a Country Churchyard' by Thomas Gray (1716–1771). This is a very soothing poem, in that the poet has a deep appreciation of what has happened during the day and of how the day has closed. The poet has an innate appreciation of his environment and surroundings – accepting the perfection of 'what is'. This work's beautiful sense of being is therefore also very healing for me. The poet's reflective mood incorporates the context of being written from within a churchyard and in turn that particular environment affects what is written and his deeply appreciative reflections and very personal observations of his community.

Merimeri Penfold

Elegy Written in a Country Churchyard

The curfew tolls the knell of parting day,
　　The lowing herd winds slowly o'er the lea,
The ploughman homeward plods his weary way,
　　And leaves the world to darkness and to me.

Now fades the glimmering landscape on the sight,
　　And all the air a solemn stillness holds,
Save where the beetle wheels his droning flight,
　　And drowsy tinklings lull the distant folds;

Save that from yonder ivy-mantled tower
　　The moping owl does to the moon complain
Of such as, wandering near her secret bower,
　　Molest her ancient solitary reign.

Beneath those rugged elms, that yew-tree's shade,
　　Where heaves the turf in many a mouldering heap,
Each in his narrow cell for ever laid,
　　The rude forefathers of the hamlet sleep.

The breezy call of incense-breathing Morn,
　　The swallow twittering from the strawbuilt shed,
The cock's shrill clarion, or the echoing horn,
　　No more shall rouse them from their lowly bed.

For them no more the blazing hearth shall burn,
　　Or busy housewife ply her evening care;
No children run to lisp their sire's return,
　　Or climb his knees the envied kiss to share.

Oft did the harvest to their sickle yield,
　　Their furrow oft the stubborn glebe has broke;
How jocund did they drive their team afield!
　　How bow'd the wood beneath their sturdy stroke!

Let not Ambition mock their useful toil,
　　Their homely joys, and destiny obscure;
Nor Grandeur hear with a disdainful smile,
　　The short and simple annals of the poor.

The boast of heraldry, the pomp of power,
　　And all that beauty, all that wealth e'er gave,
Awaits alike the inevitable hour:
　　The paths of glory lead but to the grave.

Nor you, ye proud, impute to these the fault,
　　If Memory o'er their tomb no trophies raise,
Where through the long-drawn aisle and fretted vault
　　The pealing anthem swells the note of praise.

Can storied urn or animated bust
　　Back to its mansion call the fleeting breath?
Can Honour's voice provoke the silent dust,
　　Or Flattery soothe the dull cold ear of Death?

Perhaps in this neglected spot is laid
　　Some heart once pregnant with celestial fire;
Hands that the rod of empire might have swayed,
　　Or waked to ecstasy the living lyre.

But Knowledge to their eyes her ample page
　　Rich with the spoils of time did ne'er unroll;
Chill Penury repressed their noble rage,
　　And froze the genial current of the soul.

Full many a gem of purest ray serene,
    The dark unfathomed caves of ocean bear;
Full many a flower is born to blush unseen,
    And waste its sweetness on the desert air.

Some village-Hampden that with dauntless breast
    The little tyrant of his fields withstood;
Some mute inglorious Milton here may rest,
    Some Cromwell guiltless of his country's blood.

The applause of listening senates to command,
    The threats of pain and ruin to despise,
To scatter plenty o'er a smiling land,
    And read their history in a nation's eyes,

Their lot forbade; nor circumscribed alone
    Their growing virtues, but their crimes confined;
Forbade to wade through slaughter to a throne,
    And shut the gates of mercy on mankind,

The struggling pangs of conscious truth to hide,
    To quench the blushes of ingenuous shame,
Or heap the shrine of Luxury and Pride
    With incense kindled at the Muse's flame.

Far from the madding crowd's ignoble strife,
    Their sober wishes never learned to stray;
Along the cool sequestered vale of life
    They kept the noiseless tenor of their way.

Yet ev'n these bones from insult to protect
    Some frail memorial still erected nigh,
With uncouth rhimes and shapeless sculpture decked,
    Implores the passing tribute of a sigh.

Their name, their years spelt by the unlettered muse,
  The place of fame and elegy supply;
And many a holy text around she strews,
  That teach the rustic moralist to die.

For who to dumb Forgetfulness a prey,
  This pleasing anxious being e'er resigned,
Left the warm precincts of the cheerful day,
  Nor cast one longing, lingering look behind?

On some fond breast the parting soul relies,
  Some pious drops the closing eye requires;
Ev'n from the tomb the voice of Nature cries,
  E'vn in our ashes live their wonted fires.

For thee, who mindful of the unhonoured Dead
  Dost in these lines their artless tale relate;
If chance, by lonely contemplation led,
  Some kindred spirit shall inquire thy fate,

Haply some hoary-headed swain may say,
  'Oft have we seen him at the peep of dawn
Brushing with hasty steps the dews away
  To meet the sun upon the upland lawn,

'There at the foot of yonder nodding beech,
  That wreathes its old fantastic roots so high,
His listless length at noontide would he stretch,
  And pore upon the brook that babbles by.

'Hard by yon wood, now smiling as in scorn,
  Muttering his wayward fancies he would rove,
Now drooping, woeful wan, like one forlorn,
  Or crazed with care, or crossed in hopeless love.

'One morn I missed him on the customed hill,
    Along the heath, and near his favourite tree;
Another came; nor yet beside the rill,
    Nor up the lawn, nor at the wood was he;

'The next with dirges due in sad array
    Slow through the church-way path we saw him borne.
Approach and read (for thou canst read) the lay,
    Graved on the stone beneath yon aged thorn.'

The EPITAPH

Here rests his head upon the lap of Earth
A youth to Fortune and to Fame unknown.
Fair Science frowned not on his humble birth,
And Melancholy marked him for her own.

Large was his bounty, and his soul sincere,
Heaven did a recompense as largely send:
He gave to Misery all he had, a tear,
He gained from Heaven ('twas all he wished) a friend.

No farther seek his merits to disclose,
Or draw his frailties from their dread abode,
(There they alike in trembling hope repose)
The bosom of his Father and his God.

THOMAS GRAY

Emily Perkins

WRITER

Dear Esther,

This is a poem I love for many reasons: its sense of the desperation in love, its bleak central joke and its pleasure in the knowledge that love is expressed not only in heart-shapes but also in the unlikeliest of forms. Michael Donaghy was an Irish–American poet who lived in London and died, aged 50, in 2004. Like all of his work, 'Liverpool' combines breadth and wit as casually as it places a Gnostic theologian in a tattoo parlour. As Donaghy says of the tattooists in this poem, mostly he does hearts: hearts and minds full of longing, pain, broken faith, cracked intelligence, anecdotal snap and the springy humour of street language. Of his many brilliant poems this is my favourite because I saw him recite it beautifully, with his musician's genius for performing, by heart.

Emily Perkins

Liverpool

Ever been tattooed? It takes a whim of iron,
takes sweating in the antiseptic-stinking parlour,
nothing to read but motorcycle magazines
before the blood-sopped cotton and, of course, the needle,
all for – at best – some Chinese dragon.
But mostly they do hearts,

hearts skewered, blurry, spurting like the Sacred Heart
on the arms of bikers and sailors.

Even in prison they get by with biro ink and broken glass,
carving hearts into their arms and shoulders.
But women's are more intimate. They hide theirs,
under shirts and jeans, in order to bestow them.

Like Tracy, who confessed she'd had hers done
one legless weekend with her ex.
Heart. Arrow. Even the bastard's initials, R.J.L.,
somewhere where it hurt, she said,
and when I asked her where, snapped 'Liverpool'.

Wherever it was, she'd had it sliced away
leaving a scar, she said, pink and glassy,
but small, and better than having his mark on her,

(that self-same mark of Valentinus,
who was flayed for love, but who never
– so the cardinals now say – existed.
Desanctified, apocryphal, like Christopher,
like the scar you never showed me, Trace,
your (   ), your ex, your 'Liverpool').

Still, when I unwrap the odd anonymous note
I let myself believe that it's from you.

MICHAEL DONAGHY

Anjum Rahman

WRITER, SPEAKER, MEMBER OF ISLAMIC WOMEN'S COUNCIL

Dear Cleo,

I chose this piece because it really resonates with me both as a child and as a mother. It corresponds to my religious beliefs: in Islam, children are believed to be given to us in trust. The ownership of them rests with God, and we are responsible for looking after His precious property with due care.

In all cultures and countries, parents place so many expectations on their children. Many parents want their children to be miniature versions of themselves, or to fulfil parental aspirations. Modern-day children are expected to excel in so many fields that they seem to have little time to be children. The tension is greater with migrant parents, who are often determined that their children must retain the essence of their original culture. These expectations and aspirations of parents often stifle children, and prevent them from finding their own path to fulfilment.

I'm reminded of a song by Bruce Springsteen from his album The River, called 'Independence Day'. In the song, a son explains to his father the need to leave his home town. In the final line the son swears he didn't mean to take his father's dreams from him. To me, this seems so sad. The following passage by Gibran reminds us that, as parents, our job is to teach our children to dream, but not to dream for them.

Anjum Rahman

From **The Prophet**

And a woman who held a babe against her bosom said,
   Speak to us of Children.
And he said:
Your children are not your children.
They are the sons and daughters of Life's longing for itself.
They come through you but not from you.
And though they are with you yet they belong not to you.

You may give them your love but not your thoughts,
For they have their own thoughts.
You may house their bodies but not their souls,
For their souls dwell in the house of tomorrow, which you
   cannot visit, not even in your dreams.
You may strive to be like them, but seek not to make them
   like you.
For life goes not backward nor tarries with yesterday.
You are the bows from which your children as living arrows
   are sent forth.
The Archer sees the mark upon the path of the infinite, and
   He bends you with His might that His arrows may go
   swift and far.
Let your bending in the Archer's hand be for gladness;
For even as He loves the arrow that flies, so He loves also
   the bow that is stable.

KAHLIL GIBRAN

Sir Paul Reeves

GOVERNOR-GENERAL OF NEW ZEALAND 1985–1990, FORMER PRIMATE
AND ARCHBISHOP OF NEW ZEALAND, CURRENT CHANCELLOR,
AUCKLAND UNIVERSITY OF TECHNOLOGY

Dear Libby,

I come back to this iconic poem frequently. It's best heard when accompanied by Douglas Lilburn's musical sequence and the opening lines are magic: 'Simply by sailing in a new direction/ You could enlarge the world.' The poem may be about Abel Tasman but it's bigger than that. It speaks to all of us. Me, with a whakapapa that takes my stream of life way out into the Pacific, I can relate to it. Probably a mixture of courage and desperation brought our ancestors to these islands but I'm glad they came over the unknown seas. We have our problems (who hasn't?) but I would sooner deal with them here rather than anywhere else. In 2001 I was asked by the family of Allen Curnow, the author of this poem, to conduct his funeral. It was a great privilege.

Sir Paul Reeves

from **Landfall in Unknown Seas**

The 300th Anniversary of the Discovery of New Zealand
by Abel Tasman, 13 December, 1642

I
Simply by sailing in a new direction
You could enlarge the world.

                                    You picked your captain,
Keen on discoveries, tough enough to make them,
Whatever vessels could be spared from other
More urgent service for a year's adventure;
Took stock of the more probable conjectures
About the Unknown to be traversed, all
Guesses at golden coasts and tales of monsters
To be digested into plain instructions
For likely and unlikely situations.

All this resolved and done, you launched the whole
On a fine morning, the best time of year,
Skies widening and the oceanic furies
Subdued by summer illumination; time
To go and to be gazed at going
On a fine morning, in the Name of God
Into the nameless waters of the world . . .

II
Suddenly exhilaration
Went off like a gun, the whole
Horizon, the long chase done,
Hove to. There was the seascape
Crammed with coast, surprising
As new lands will, the sailor
Moving on the face of the waters,
Watching the earth take shape

Round the unearthly summits, brighter
Than its emerging colour . . .

III
. . . But now there are no more islands to be found
And the eye scans risky horizons of its own
In unsettled weather, and murmurs of the drowned
    Haunt their familiar beaches —
Who navigate us towards what unknown

But not improbable provinces? Who reaches
A future down for us from the high shelf
Of spiritual daring? Not those speeches
    Pinning on the Past like a decoration
For merit that congratulates itself,

O not the self-important celebration
Or most painstaking history, can release
The current of a discoverer's elation
    And silence the voices saying,
'Here is the world's end where wonders cease'.

Only by a more faithful memory, laying
On him the half-light of a diffident glory,
The Sailor lives, and stands beside us, paying
    Out into our time's wave
The stain of blood that writes an island story.

ALLEN CURNOW

Last Evenings on Earth

JOHN REYNOLDS

John Reynolds

ARTIST

Dear Esther,

'A strange light descended on us tonight' begins Kapka
Kassabova's flaring poem, 'Glimpses of Ecstasy over the Pacific'.
I immediately find myself at dusk on the hillside above Whites
Beach on Auckland's west coast.

Glimpses, strange light, ecstasy: already we are regarding
'the way of all sunsets'.

By way of response to this searching work, I felt a recent
painting of mine, *Last Evenings on Earth*, seemed to best
track the poem's descending chords.

> Oceans from a plane?
> Years unfolding like maps?

Somehow the painting's bold slew and Kassabova's 'stupor
of transience' seem to be regarding similar vistas.

Good luck with it all,

John

Glimpses of Ecstasy over the Pacific

A strange light descended on us tonight.
The concrete promenade
became a secret path

The harbour rainbow was the contour
of some extravagant design
we couldn't grasp

The sea-rocks turned towards the moon
like silver-foil reflection
of a world that could be ours

if only we believed in it.
And that is the problem:
believing is more than seeing

I kept walking and watching
the miracle shrink behind the hills,
which is the way of all sunsets

but this one was different,
this one felt as if
the last of something would be gone

Some stopped and watched
to keep it longer, while others were afraid
of endings, and kept their backs to it –

the man in shorts and pulled-up socks,
for instance, his legs the arch
where middle age slumps into old

And suddenly, like him, I was removed
from my best life, here at the centre
of some old, awful truth, and I walked

behind the moving sky
in a stupor of transience,
in a slow motion of fear

unsure how much time
remained to me, and how to measure it
In perfect evenings? Outbreaks of sky? Hope, beauty?

Oceans from a plane?
Years unfolding like maps?
I ran to catch it, I needed to know

Then it was gone behind the hill.
Left in semi-darkness, we continued
our crab-like scuttle to the dawn

KAPKA KASSABOVA

Margi Robertson

FASHION DESIGNER, NOM*D

Dear Cleo,

When I first heard Nick Cave's music, his words portrayed an image of a dark obsession with love and death, ballads that sang of all the woes of life in the most beautiful poetic way.

There were so many of his works I could have chosen, especially the Love Songs, however this one has always been a favourite.

So sad and tragic and beautiful.

Cheers,

Margi

The Weeping Song

Go son, go down to the water
And see the women weeping there
Then go up into the mountains
The men, they are weeping too

Father, why are all the women weeping?
They are weeping for their men
Then why are all the men there weeping?
They are weeping back at them

This is a weeping song
A song in which to weep
While all the men and women sleep
This is a weeping song
But I won't be weeping long

Father, why are all the children weeping?
They are merely crying son
O, are they merely crying, father?
Yes, true weeping is yet to come

This is a weeping song
A song in which to weep
While all the men and women sleep
This is a weeping song
But I won't be weeping long

O father tell me, are you weeping?
Your face seems wet to touch
O then I'm so sorry, father
I never thought I hurt you so much

This is a weeping song
A song in which to weep
While we rock ourselves to sleep
This is a weeping song
But I won't be weeping long
But I won't be weeping long
But I won't be weeping long
But I won't be weeping long

NICK CAVE

Mark Sainsbury

PRESENTER, *CLOSE UP*

Dear Libby,

Deciding my favourite poet was easy. Sam Hunt when I was growing up was the man who made it okay to be into poetry. Not only was he an extraordinary figure in himself, his writing was something again. I have many Sam favourites, but 'Beware the Man' gets to me on all sorts of levels. When I first heard it, it resonated in the spirit of the times, we all of course were suspicious of the man, and felt we were so very very special with insight no other generation ever had.

As the years have rolled by it still resonates but from differing perspectives and I found as I moved into journalism that it had a particular significance. So this is my poem for all seasons and a constant reminder not be fitted into anyone else's idea of conformity.

I had until a few years ago a very tangible reminder of this poem. After I heard it the first time I went out and bought a black hat: I thought I was so cool. The hat has finally gone; the poem is with me for ever.

Mark Sainsbury

Beware the Man

Beware the man who tries to fit you out
In his idea of a hat
Dictating the colour and the shape of it.

He takes your head and carefully measures it
says 'Of course black's out',
He sees himself in the big black hat.

So you may be a member of the act
He makes for you your special coloured hat.
Beware! He's fitting you for more than that.

SAM HUNT

Susan St John

ECONOMIST, CHILD POVERTY ACTION GROUP COMMITTEE MEMBER

Dear Cleo,

I love how Wordsworth shows us how growing into 'the common light of day' of the adult world causes a disconnection from what we instinctively understood in childhood. To see my new granddaughter 'trailing clouds of glory' as she sleeps without any imprint of worldly care is to be transported to that magical time when even common, everyday things were 'apparelled in celestial light', as one of the opening lines of this long poem expresses it. The madness of the world today with its technological weaponry and ancient enmities contrasts starkly with the serenity of the infinite. The challenge of growing older is to seek through 'the noisy years' a reconnection with the 'immortal sea', and to make sure all our children can experience for as long as possible that blissful state of infancy.

Susan St John

from Ode: Intimations of Immortality
from Recollections of Early Childhood

V
Our birth is but a sleep and a forgetting:
The Soul that rises with us, our life's Star,
    Hath had elsewhere its setting,
        And cometh from afar:
    Not in entire forgetfulness,
    And not in utter nakedness,
But trailing clouds of glory do we come

From God, who is our home:
Heaven lies about us in our infancy!
Shades of the prison-house begin to close
    Upon the growing Boy,
But He beholds the light, and whence it flows,
    He sees it in his joy;
The Youth, who daily farther from the east
    Must travel, still is Nature's Priest,
    And by the vision splendid
    Is on his way attended;
At length the Man perceives it die away,
And fade into the light of common day.

IX

. . . Our noisy years seem moments in the being
Of the eternal Silence: truths that wake,
    To perish never:
Which neither listlessness, nor mad endeavour,
    Nor Man nor Boy,
Nor all that is at enmity with joy,
Can utterly abolish or destroy!
Hence in a season of calm weather
    Though inland far we be,
Our Souls have sight of that immortal sea
    Which brought us hither,
    Can in a moment travel thither,
And see the Children sport upon the shore,
And hear the mighty waters rolling evermore.

WILLIAM WORDSWORTH

Anand Satyanand

GOVERNOR-GENERAL OF NEW ZEALAND

Dear Esther,

I enjoy this poem because it is an instant distillation of New Zealand imagery, with words such as casual, country, Maori, connection between races, interdependence, spirituality and hope all coming to mind. James K. Baxter was a European New Zealander who could empathise with things Maori in an inimitable fashion.

Anand Satyanand

A Pair of Sandals

A pair of sandals, old black pants
And leather coat – I must go, my friends,
Into the dark, the cold, the first beginning
Where the ribs of the ancestor are the rafters
Of a meeting house – windows broken
And the floor white with bird dung – in there
The ghosts gather who will instruct me
And when the river fog rises
Te ra rite tonu te Atua –
The sun who is like the Lord
Will warm my bones, and his arrows
Will pierce to the centre of the shapeless clay of the mind.

JAMES K. BAXTER

Tom Scott

CARTOONIST

Dear Libby,

It's short, bitter-sweet and true. The main reason we all need to be numerate is so we can count our blessings.

Tom Scott

Carrington Briggs

Carrington Briggs
Cared not two figs
whether he lived or died
But when he was dead
he sat on his bed
and he cried and he cried
and he cried.

SPIKE MILLIGAN

Tim Shadbolt

MAYOR, INVERCARGILL

Dear Va,

Many war heroes have written anti-war poetry, but I doubt that any wrote their poems while in prison for murder.

This poem was given to me by Colonel Awatere while I was in Mt Eden prison for saying 'bullshit' in a public place. It was published in the *PD Barb* in 1969.

Yours sincerely,

Tim Shadbolt

What Price Vietnam

We are a true sov'reign Nation,
Our creed is western democracy;
Freedom from fear and from want,
Freedom of worship and speech,
Into our live world economy
Into our live social ways,
Moulding our live way of life.
Name it? It is plain Nationalism!

We are true sov'reign Nation,
Moulded of fine ethnic groups:
Each one internally fortified
By its traditional identity,
By its traditional affinity,
By its own in-group serenity:

Sinews of our sov'reign Nation,
Bound by our live Nationalism!

We are all happy to live it
Free of disturbance, annoyance,
Free of some odd interference
By some brash meddling Nations:
Free from the fear of domination,
Free from the fear of oppression,
Free from fear of atrocities
By arrogant self-seeking Nations!

Vietnam! Ah, that name is pitiful
Know of it? Heard of it? . . . Yes?
Ancient and war-ravaged Nation!
'Live and let live' is our dictum,
Free from the rash powerful Nations,
Free from the arrogant nations.
'Guilty!' Time points out accusingly,
'Guilty, but vainly self-righteous!'

Must we be fighting in Vietnam?
Is it blackmail we are paying
For non-embargo on exports?
Which we must trade with a Nation?
Let us uphold what is right!
Let us uphold our live principles!
Let us uphold our Nationalism!
Bring back our soldiers . . . alive!

ARAPETA AWATERE

Ced Simpson

EXECUTIVE DIRECTOR, AMNESTY INTERNATIONAL
AOTEAROA NEW ZEALAND

Dear Libby

I first read this as a teenager. Like Peter Benenson, the founder of Amnesty International, I was raised a Catholic. Growing up I was struck by the concern for the poor and marginalised shown in the Christian gospel and could not help contrasting this with the pomp, splendour and hypocrisy of some of those professing to be Christian. In the poem, published in 1633 after his death, clergyman George Herbert appears to be seeking out his God to cut a new deal. He finds Him, not in a heavenly palace, nor in places of wealth, power and influence, but in the form of a dying human being amidst thieves and murderers.

Ced Simpson

Redemption

Having been tenant long to a rich Lord,
    Not thriving, I resolved to be bold,
    And make a suit unto him, to afford
A new small-rented lease, and cancell th' old.

In heaven at his manour I him sought:
    They told me there, that he was lately gone
    About some land, which he had dearly bought
Long since on earth, to take possession.

I straight return'd, and knowing his great birth,
    Sought him accordingly in great resorts;
    In cities, theatres, gardens, parks, and courts :
At length I heard a ragged noise and mirth

    Of theeves and murderers: there I him espied,
    Who straight, *Your suit is granted*, said, and died.

GEORGE HERBERT

Stephen Sinclair

PLAYWRIGHT, SCREENWRITER, POET

Dear Geraldine,

The poem I have chosen is 'Sailing to Byzantium,' by W.B.
Yeats. I don't really have one favourite poem, but this certainly
makes the short list. I learned it by heart when I was a teenager,
and still find it beautiful and moving every time I read or recite
it. If anything it has more meaning for me now than it did
then; having turned 50 I can empathise all too readily with its
lament for lost youth and the advance of bodily decrepitude!
Yeats sought to create from these feelings something of
imperishable beauty. He certainly achieved this here and with
many other poems. I hope it gives you and your classmates as
much pleasure as it has me for so many years.

Regards,

Stephen Sinclair

Sailing to Byzantium

I
That is no country for old men. The young
In one another's arms, birds in the trees,
– Those dying generations – at their song,
The salmon-falls, the mackerel-crowded seas,
Fish, flesh, or fowl, commend all summer long
Whatever is begotten, born, and dies.
Caught in that sensual music all neglect
Monuments of unageing intellect.

II

An aged man is but a paltry thing,
A tattered coat upon a stick, unless
Soul clap its hands and sing, and louder sing
For every tatter in its mortal dress,
Nor is there singing school but studying
Monuments of its own magnificence;
And therefore I have sailed the seas and come
To the holy city of Byzantium.

III

O sages standing in God's holy fire
As in the gold mosaic of a wall,
Come from the holy fire, perne in a gyre,
And be the singing-masters of my soul.
Consume my heart away; sick with desire
And fastened to a dying animal
It knows not what it is; and gather me
Into the artifice of eternity.

IV

Once out of nature I shall never take
My bodily form from any natural thing,
But such a form as Grecian goldsmiths make
Of hammered gold and gold enamelling
To keep a drowsy Emperor awake;
Or set upon a golden bough to sing
To lords and ladies of Byzantium
Of what is past, or passing, or to come.

W.B. YEATS

Elizabeth Smither

POET

Dear Libby and Lisa,

Thank you for inviting me to contribute to *Dear to Me*. I was a member of Amnesty for many years so I am particularly delighted.

I like this poem for its prescription of love and what it should be: either a coming together, or, if love fades, a mutual retirement. Love demands mutuality, not one partner hankering for love after it has cooled or vanished, or one loving another who cannot return love, or longing for a vanished love. What is gone is gone, it seems to say, and the process must begin at once.

> Well, now,
> if little by little you stop loving me
> I shall stop loving you little by little.

How wise that is, and how hard to learn: not to waste one's life on what cannot be returned but beat a gracious and simultaneous retreat. 'But' — and the poem contains this wonderful *but* — which is the other side of the coin, the returning motion —

> if each day,
> each hour,
> you feel that you are destined for me

then comes the lovely image of the flower and the passionate reward of the last lines, 'my love feeds on your love' and the intertwined arms.

The wind of banners is lovely too – the unknown that passes
through a life bringing change – but loveliest of all is the
knowledge that the roots of the heart can set off in another
direction and after long slow change, not be defeated.

Very best wishes for your project,

Elizabeth Smither

If You Forget Me

I want you to know
one thing.

You know how this is:
if I look
at the crystal moon, at the red branch
of the slow autumn at my window,
if I touch
near the fire
the impalpable ash
or the wrinkled body of the log,
everything carries me to you,
as if everything that exists,
aromas, light, metals,
were little boats that sail
toward those isles of yours that wait for me.

Well, now,
if little by little you stop loving me
I shall stop loving you little by little.

If suddenly
you forget me
do not look for me,
for I shall already have forgotten you.

If you think it long and mad,
the wind of banners
that passes through my life,
and you decide
to leave me at the shore
of the heart where I have roots,
remember
that on that day,
at that hour,
I shall lift my arms
and my roots will set off
to seek another land.

But
if each day,
each hour,
you feel that you are destined for me
with implacable sweetness,
if each day a flower
climbs up to your lips to seek me,
ah my love, ah my own,
in me all that fire is repeated,
in me nothing is extinguished or forgotten,
my love feeds on your love, beloved,
and as long as you live it will be in your arms
without leaving mine.

PABLO NERUDA

C.K. Stead

WRITER

Dear Shika,

I am not choosing an easy poem, but an exceptionally strong
one which lodged in my head when I read it, many times, more
than half a century ago, and remains there today. What I find
remarkable about John Donne's 'A Nocturnal upon St Lucy's
Day' is its strict formal control, its tight structure of thought,
and yet, driving like a bulldozer through all of that, its passion.
The form is very precise: nine-line stanzas rhyming a b b a c c
c d d, with lines 1, 2, 6, 7, 8 and 9 iambic pentameters, lines 3
and 4 iambic tetrameters, and line 5 an iambic trimeter. The
governing idea is that we have come to the shortest, darkest
day of the year, after which the world will climb back towards
light and spring and warmth and young love. But because of
his loss (the woman he loves has died) the poet, or his persona
(the person he is pretending to be), knows that he will not
recover; that he has become a perfect negative, less than a
shadow, a nothing, fit only for death. Read aloud, the force of
this idea, and the emotional charge the lines contain, reaching
their great crescendo in the opening of the final stanza

> But I am none; nor will my sun renew

impose another form — the form of the emotion — upon the
mere count of syllables and the recognition of rhyme. This,
I think, is a measure of what poetry in the English language
can do at its very best: but like most poetry of that period
(Shakespeare's too) it is written for the ear as well as for the
eye, and must be heard aloud for its full force to be felt.

I have modernised the spellings in the attached copy.

I wish you all the best with this excellent project.

Yours sincerely,

Karl Stead

A Nocturnal upon St Lucy's Day
Being the Shortest Day

'Tis the year's midnight, and it is the day's,
Lucy's, who scarce seven hours herself unmasks;
    The sun is spent, and now his flasks
    Send forth light squibs, no constant rays;
      The world's whole sap is sunk:
The general balm th'hydroptic earth hath drunk,
Whither, as to the bed's feet life is shrunk,
Dead and interred: yet all these seem to laugh
Compar'd with me, who am their epitaph.

Study me then you who shall lovers be
At the next world, that is at the next spring:
    For I am every dead thing
    In whom love wrought new alchemy.
      For his art did express
A quintessence even from nothingness,
From dull privations and lean emptiness:
He ruin'd me, and I am re-begot
Of absence, darkness, death; things which are not.

All others, from all things, draw all that's good,
Life, soul, form, spirit, whence they being have;
  I, by love's limbeck, am the grave
  Of all that's nothing. Oft a flood
   Have we two wept, and so
Drown'd the whole world, us two; oft did we grow
To be two chaoses, when we did show
Care to ought else; and often absences
Withdrew our souls and made us carcasses.

But I am by her death, (which word wrongs her)
Of the first nothing the Elixir grown;
  Were I a man, that I were one
  I needs must know; I should prefer
   If I were any beast
Some ends, some means; yea plants, yea stones, detest
And love; all, all some properties invest;
If I an ordinary nothing were
As shadow, a light and body must be here.

But I am none, nor will my sun renew.
You lovers, for whose sake the lesser sun
  At this time to the Goat is run
  To fetch new lust and give it you,
   Enjoy your summer all;
Since she enjoys her long night's festival,
Let me prepare towards her, and let me call
This hour her Vigil, and her Eve, since this
Both the year's, and the day's, deep midnight is.

JOHN DONNE

Dougal Stevenson

RADIO AND TELEVISION PERSONALITY

Dear Libby,

I have chosen a poem by Cilla McQueen from *Markings*, published by the University of Otago Press in 2000 – it is my favourite short poem. 'Luncheon Cove' is spare, whimsical and evocative of a place echoing faintly of 'the friendless outer edge of space' that another New Zealand poet, R.A.K. Mason, described.

Cilla McQueen's poem reaches back to a time when the land had been circumnavigated but the imagination had not yet discovered New Zealand. The image of the great navigator being utterly 'British' – as if dining in London with the Royal Society, but in reality seated in one of the farthest and wettest precincts of the world, with water probably staining the linen and soaking his wig – is delicious.

Cheers, and all the best,

Dougal Stevenson

Luncheon Cove

It was so calm in Dusky Sound
that Captain Cook requested
luncheon served ashore

beside the frothing pool
of a stream tumbling out of the bush
where sunlight filtered down

and cool air sprang
from amber peaty water, edged
with rock and fern.

His linen white, his table set with silver,
Captain Cook had an eerie, solitary feeling,
as if he had set foot on the moon.

CILLA MCQUEEN

Feleti Strickson-Pua

MUSICIAN

Dear Va,

Dear to me is my son Che'den Sofi Ah Yek Strickson-Pua (four years) who created this poem 'The St Columbo's Cat' with his first cousin Jane Filemu (six years) a few years ago. This poem was then published by Che'den's papa. There's a strong family link in this story. As a composer I am grateful for Che'den and Jane creating new stories and songs. Being Che'den's dad I am very proud of his efforts. As parents we should enjoy our children and making this world a safer place for all the children. 'The St Columbo's Cat' is about our children who deserve our aroha and only the best.

Feleti Strickson-Pua

The St Columbo's Cat

The St Columbo's cat
lives in a tree
and when
we visit

He
jumps out
and
bites our knees.

The St Columbo's cat!

CHE'DEN & JANE

Grahame Sydney

PAINTER

Dear Geraldine,

The year 1986 was a tough one for me, my much-loved Dad
declining into a weak and vulnerable ghost of his former
cheery, good-natured self as the 'diabetes' he had been diag-
nosed as suffering slowly manifested itself as terminal bone
cancer. There was nothing we could do but watch this cruel
and painful decline, and I took it terribly hard. The helplessness
I felt was nothing to what he must have been feeling, and I was
angry, too, that at only 74 years, my dad was being unfairly
taken from our lives.

He died in a hospital bedroom at a very early pre-dawn hour,
with the family beside him. I went home as dawn began
to colour the night sky that December morning, and having
phoned a couple of close friends to tell them the sad news,
tried to sleep. In the letterbox a few hours later I found an
unstamped envelope with my name on it, in a handwriting
I recognised: Brian Turner's. The envelope contained this
beautiful poem, so poignant and so comforting still, written
for my dead father, and me.

Grahame Sydney

After

(for Grahame)

The dead do
sing in us, in
us and through
us, and to themselves
under their mounds of earth
swelling in the sun, or in their
ashes that shine
as they depart on the wind.

See how the grass
sways to the sound
of their voices
under, singing
the beautiful
eternal sadness
of before
relieved of the
resolve of after.

BRIAN TURNER

Marte Szirmay

SCULPTOR

Dear Va and Libby,

Thank you for the invitation to participate in the *Dear to Me* project.

The poem I have selected from my collection of favourites is one I first came across in 1974 as a young woman. It is one of Kevin Ireland's Literary Cartoons: 'The Literary Man Tends a Modern Garden'. At the time I first discovered it, I was heavily involved with the Vietnam protests and the anti-nuclear movement. The poem's simplicity and poignancy immediately gave a voice to our global reality viewed from this far-away land of milk & honey. I have never forgotten the poem during all these years for there has been little respite in the 'bleeding of that far-off part of creation' . . . and I keep asking what has changed?

All the best for a successful publication,

Marte Szirmay

The Literary Man Tends a Modern Garden

shots were being fired
while he weeded the flower-bed
a soldier joined the glorious dead
his arms and back felt tired

he forked over the compost pit
a bomber glinted overhead
he stopped for tea and raisin-bread
a school was blown to bits

as he raked and trimmed and dug
some shabby village fled
a far-off part of creation bled
he ground his heel on a slug

he spread a plot with potash
a paddyfield ran red
he stacked his garden tools in the shed
chill sunset flared like a gunflash

KEVIN IRELAND

John Tamihere

BROADCASTER, FORMER MP

Dear Libby,

This poem by James K. Baxter has always interested and fascinated me. Baxter was and is a part of Kiwi folklore. He along with others of his generation embarked upon a 'Kiwi-isation' of literature. The advance guard of writing in a way that captured New Zealanders at work, at play, in love, at war and just being Kiwis.

'Ballad of Calvary Street' captures a generation of Kiwis. It examines the pre-MMP politics and the tribal nature of the two teams that participated; 'National Mum and Labour Dad'. It defines the quintessential Kiwi family from Sunday gatherings to the mandatory garden out the back. It touches on our collective morality, from affairs to staying in the marriage regardless of whether Yin and Yang would ever meet in Calvary Street.

Above all it connects and, as a poem, reaches out to me using a language, a cadence and storytelling that only a Kiwi exposed to this period can rejoice in and celebrate.

John Tamihere

Ballad of Calvary Street

On Calvary Street are trellises
Where bright as blood the roses bloom,
And gnomes like pagan fetishes
Hang their hats on an empty tomb

Where two old souls go slowly mad,
National Mum and Labour Dad.

Each Saturday when full of smiles
The children come to pay their due,
Mum takes down the family files
And cover to cover she thumbs them through,
Poor Len before he went away
And Mabel on her wedding day.

The meal-brown scones display her knack,
Her polished oven spits with rage,
While in Grunt Grotto at the back
Dad sits and reads the Sporting Page,
Then ambles out in boots of lead
To weed around the parsnip bed.

A giant parsnip sparks his eye,
Majestic as the Tree of Life;
He washes it and rubs it dry
And takes it in to his old wife –
'Look Laura, would that be a fit?
The bastard has a flange on it!'

When both were young she would have laughed,
A goddess in her tartan skirt,
But wisdom, age and mothercraft
Have rubbed it home that men like dirt:
Five children and a fallen womb,
A golden crown beyond the tomb.

Nearer the bone, sin is sin,
And women bear the cross of woe,
And that affair with Mrs Flynn

(It happened thirty years ago)
Though never mentioned, means that he
Will get no sugar in his tea.

The afternoon goes by, goes by,
The angels harp above a cloud;
A son-in-law with spotted tie
And daughter Alice fat and loud
Discuss the virtues of insurance
And stuff their tripes with trained endurance.

Flood-waters hurl upon the dyke
And Dad himself can go to town,
For little Charlie on his trike
Has ploughed another iris down.
His parents rise to chain the beast,
Brush off the last crumbs of their lovefeast.

And so these two old fools are left,
A rosy pair in evening light,
To question Heaven's dubious gift,
To hag and grumble, growl and fight:
The love they kill won't let them rest,
Two birds that peck in one fouled nest.

Why hammer nails? Why give no change?
Habit, habit clogs them dumb.
The Sacred Heart above the range
Will bleed and burn till Kingdom Come,
But Yin and Yang won't ever meet
In Calvary Street, in Calvary Street.

JAMES K. BAXTER

Georgina te Heuheu

MEMBER OF PARLIAMENT

Dear Geraldine,

Thank you for inviting me to participate in this exciting project, *Dear to Me*. I welcome the opportunity to support Amnesty International in this way.

Having loved poetry since I was a child, choosing a favourite poem is a real challenge. I studied poetry through to university, at which time English and American poetry illuminated my world. Later, our own New Zealand poets emerged to add an even richer layer of understanding and appreciation of that world, particularly of ourselves and our lives here in Aotearoa.

I have chosen 'Papa-tu-a-nuku (Earth Mother)' by Hone Tuwhare, whose work I greatly admire. He is an icon among icons. I have had the privilege of seeing him reading his work, and have listened in awe. I love reading his poetry and often do so out loud, to myself.

Tuwhare uses language to fully engage all of the reader's senses. 'Papa-tu-a-nuku (Earth Mother)' is a perfect example of his genius. It is simple, yet provocative; a work of beauty and passion. It hooks the reader in a mischievous but loving way. Written with reference to a landmark event in our nation's history – The Awakening; the Maori Land March of 1975 – it serves to illuminate the significance of that event by placing it in the context of a simple, but equally significant, relationship; that of Earth Mother and her children (ourselves). We cannot help but love her!

Best wishes,

Hon Georgina te Heuheu QSO

Papa-tu-a-nuku (Earth Mother)

We are stroking, caressing the spine
    of the land.

We are massaging the ricked
    back of the land

with our sore but ever-loving feet:
    hell, she loves it!

Squirming, the land wriggles
    in delight.

    We love her.

HONE TUWHARE

Dame Catherine Tizard

GOVERNOR-GENERAL OF NEW ZEALAND 1990–1996

Dear Cleo,

Thank you for the invitation to be part of your *Dear to Me* project. I am happy to participate and do this little thing to support Amnesty.

I hope you feel that a tongue-in-cheek poem by a New Zealand poet will be appropriate. I have always had a soft spot for Rex Fairburn and his work. This was, I think, the last poem he had published in the *Listener* before his death. I knew Rex as a fellow party-goer back in the 1950s and he was my English tutor at Auckland University. In his laconic, informal way, he opened our minds and imaginations without, I think, even consciously trying. He talked with us, not at us.

Why do I choose this – out of all his many poems? I like its mock-lament; its self-mockery; the not-so-sly digs at poetic pretentions and also the fact that it is a send-up of the rather pompous Thomas Bracken poem of a previous age.

Just the same, there is a serious, even bitter, undertone lamenting the cultural desert that was the New Zealand of those times. Writing was assumed to be a part-time, self-indulgent hobby and writers, certainly poets, were expected to have 'real jobs' – and they did. They had to. How much, I wonder, has really changed?

Fairburn's work has been somewhat neglected but in the past few years there has been an upsurge of interest and appreciation of his wonderful talent, giving him his rightful place as a major New Zealand poet.

Thank you for supporting Amnesty,

Cath Tizard

Not Understood

(For the Secret Brotherhood, with a bouquet
of ragwort and bracken)

Not understood. We move along asunder,
    The mists get thicker as our syntax goes,
And in the fog we marvel and we wonder
    That any line we write, in verse or prose,
        Is understood.

Not understood. We bury all our meanings,
    And dig them deeper as the years go by,
Indulging thus our obscurantist leanings;
    And it will be no wonder if we die
        Not understood.

Not understood. Despondency and madness
    Attend us as communications fail;
We poets in our youth begin in gladness,
    But end in Paul's or Whitcombe's Christmas sale,
        Not understood.

Not understood. Our tendency is laudable,
    Uttering, for elevation of our thought,
In thick sonorous voices, quite inaudible
    To the vast multitude; our books unbought,
        Not understood.

Not understood. The reading mob's reaction
   To what it does not comprehend is slow,
And gives small hope. But with self-satisfaction
   We judge our verses, though they often go
      Not understood.

Not understood. Poor souls with stunted vision
   Oft measure giants by their narrow gauge;
The poisoned shafts of falsehood and derision
   Are oft impelled 'gainst us who mould the age,
      Not understood.

Not understood! How many hearts are aching
   For poems that are plain, and language terse!
The poetry you write is epoch-making,
   Yet, wanting the accomplishment of verse,
      Not understood.

Oh, God! that bards could be a little clearer,
   Or write less often when they've nowt to say;
Oh, God! that bards would live a little nearer
   To us, and in the light of common day,
      Not under Milk Wood.

A.R.D. FAIRBURN

Jools and Lynda Topp

SINGER–SONGWRITERS, ENTERTAINERS

Dear Cleo,

Growing up on the farm, the paddocks were our playground, and like all kids, we noticed everything that went on. Cows are very affectionate animals, and although there was no bull around, they displayed a lot of physical affection for each other. I guess we related to what we observed . . . you know the cows are like us too!

Observation and relating to what you see going on can help you make sense of the world.

Jools and Lynda

Cows

Well I'm a dyke from way back in the country off a farm
And I've got a farming yarn
Ooh near long as your arm

Cows are matriarchal and as dykish as can be
And I've got some facts to back this up
Cos I've studied this at length
And I think the facts I've got
Have got a lot of strength

For a start cows live together
And their communal spirit's high
And when they sleep and eat and drink together
It brings a dyke tear to my eye

Now dog's a man's best friend
so says the species man
But a cow can't be a man's best friend
Cos she'll kick him if she can
And just to show she loathes him so
She'll smash the gate or rush his dog
Or won't let her milk ————— go

And in all the years
I've known cows
As sure as sheep have wool
I've never met a cow
Who jumped the fence
To see the Bull.

THE TOPP TWINS

Chris Trotter

POLITICAL JOURNALIST, COMMENTATOR

Dear Libby,

James K. Baxter's 'Crossing Cook Strait' has always been
something of a manifesto for me. Since first reading it in my
late teens, the poem has never failed to challenge me to think
about the state of our nation and my duty as a citizen. The
poet's choice of the inter-island ferry as the vehicle for 'the
terrestrial journey/From chaos into light' immediately caught
my imagination. I, too, had travelled the Strait by night; felt the
surge of the ship through the water; and wondered where, and
to what, it was taking me. As the poem unfolds it becomes clear
that the ferry is in fact the New Zealand ship of state, and that
the poet/reader is confronting the nation's tutelary deity –
brilliantly conceived as 'Seddon and Savage, the socialist
father'. He chides us for our lack of love, our selfishness, and
for the slow death of our civic spirit. Like Baxter, we are roused
to do our duty – only to have the elusive spirit of history
abandon us with an 'ambiguous salute'. But by then, of course,
the spell is well and truly cast. Baxter has bludgeoned us alive
with his verse to our 'peril and purpose', and we are no longer
free to ignore the shouts of the 'angry poor' for 'bread and
justice'. For my money, it is, quite simply, the finest political
poem New Zealand has produced.

Chris Trotter

Crossing Cook Strait

The night was clear, sea calm; I came on deck
To stretch my legs, find perhaps
Gossip, a girl in green slacks at the rail
Or just the logline feathering a dumb wake.

The ship swung in the elbow of the Strait.
'Dolphins!' I cried — 'let the true sad Venus
Rise riding her shoals, teach me as once to wonder
And wander at ease, be glad and never regret.'

But night increased under the signal stars.
In the dark bows, facing the flat sea,
Stood one I had not expected, yet knew without surprise
As the Janus made formidable by loveless years.

His coat military; his gesture mild —
'Well met,' he said, 'on the terrestrial journey
From chaos into light — what light it is
Contains our peril and purpose, history has not revealed.'

'Sir —', I began. He spoke with words of steel —
'I am Seddon and Savage, the socialist father.
You have known me only in my mask of Dionysus
Amputated in bar rooms, dismembered among wheels.

'I woke in my civil tomb hearing a shout
For bread and justice. It was not here.
That sound came thinly over the waves from China;
Stones piled on my grave had all but shut it out.

'I walked forth gladly to find the angry poor
Who are my nation; discovered instead

The glutton seagulls squabbling over crusts
And policies made and broken behind locked doors.

'I have watched the poets also at their trade.
I have seen them burning with wormwood brilliance.
Love was the one thing lacking on their page,
The crushed herb of grief at another's pain.

'Your civil calm breeds inward poverty
That chafes for change. The ghost of Adam
Gibbering demoniac in drawing-rooms
Will drink down hemlock with his sugared tea.

'You feed your paupers concrete. They work well,
Ask for no second meal, vote, pay tribute
Of silence on Anzac Day in the pub urinal;
Expose death only by a mushroom smell.

'My counsel was naïve. Anger is bread
To the poor, their guns more accurate than justice,
Because their love has not decayed to a wintry fungus
And hope to the wish for power among the dead.

'In Kaitangata the miner's falling sweat
Wakes in the coal seams fossil flowers.
The clerk puts down his pen and takes his coat;
He will not be back today or the next day either.'

With an ambiguous salute he left me.
The ship moved into a stronger sea,
Bludgeoned alive by the rough mystery
Of love in the running straits of history.

JAMES K. BAXTER

Brian Turner

POET, SPORTSMAN

Dear Shika,

I have scores of so-called 'favourite' poems, but this one strikes
me as a beauty: near-perfect pitch and tone, and right the way
through it's measured, discreet, subtle, poignant. I love the
choice of verbs: 'The wind distresses tail and mane'; 'distances
. . . fable them'; 'names were artificed'; 'Dusk brims the
shadows', and so on. There are unexpected and apt
observations, among them 'stop-press columns on the street'
and an absence of 'stop-watch prophesies'. All through it's
implied that beauty and fame, say, are temporary, and all –
humans included – have their heyday and its aftermath.
Everything steals away 'but the unmolesting meadows'. But that
doesn't mean there's an absence of 'joy' even though in the end
there's 'Only the groom, and the groom's boy,/With bridles in
the evening . . .' Precise, simple-seeming but not simple, plain-
seeming but not so plain, clear yet subtle, Larkin, at his best,
knew what he was doing and how to do it.

Good wishes,

Brian Turner

At Grass

The eye can hardly pick them out
From the cold shade they shelter in,
Till wind distresses tail and mane;
Then one crops grass, and moves about
– The other seeming to look on –
And stands anonymous again.

Yet fifteen years ago, perhaps
Two dozen distances sufficed
To fable them: faint afternoons
Of Cups and Stakes and Handicaps,
Whereby their names were artificed
To inlay faded, classic Junes —

Silks at the start: against the sky
Numbers and parasols: outside,
Squadrons of empty cars, and heat,
And littered grass: then the long cry
Hanging unhushed till it subside
To stop-press columns on the street.

Do memories plague their ears like flies?
They shake their heads. Dusk brims the shadows.
Summer by summer all stole away,
The starting-gates, the crowds and cries —
All but the unmolesting meadows.
Almanacked, their names live; they

Have slipped their names, and stand at ease,
Or gallop for what must be joy,
And not a fieldglass sees them home,
Or curious stop-watch prophesies:
Only the groom, and the groom's boy,
With bridles in the evening come.

PHILIP LARKIN

Glenn Turner

CRICKETER

Greetings Lisa,

I am happy to accept your invitation. The poem I have selected
is from Brian Turner's *Taking Off* and is called 'Cricket'.

It seems that just about everyone who follows sport confesses
to having an expert knowledge of the subject. The nature of
cricket (more than most games) has enough variables to
encourage a wide range of opinions. Brian Turner's poem
expresses this very cleverly and succinctly.

Good luck with your project.

Cheers,

Glenn Turner

Cricket

A game about which
you can know very little
and say anything
and be right sooner or later.

BRIAN TURNER

Ranginui Walker

ACADEMIC

Dear Libby,

I love this lament from the people of Tainui. It is sung to a
haunting melody that is expressive of the sentiments that
'parting is such sweet sorrow', and 'to part is to die a little'. It
is usually sung as a complement to an orator's speech. It is a
fitting lament to farewell the dead at a tangihanga (funeral).

Ranginui Walker

E Pa To Hau

E pa to hau he wini raro,
He homai aroha ka tangi atu au i konei,
He aroha ki te iwi ka momotu ki tawhiti ki Paerau,
Ko wai e kite atu kei whea aku hoa i mua ra,
I te tonuitanga, ka haeremai tenei ka tauwehe
Ka raungaiti au i.

The wind carries tidings of you from the North,
It bears your love and I lament from here,
In sorrow for the people who were exiled afar to Paerau.
Who will see again my friends of yore?
When in prosperous times we were parted,
And I am left bereft.

Wendy Walker

CLINICAL DIRECTOR, KIDZ FIRST CHILDREN'S HOSPITAL
AND COMMUNITY HEALTH

Dear Cleo,

As a paediatrician and a mother, I think poetry for children is very important. I have always loved *Hairy Maclary from Donaldson's Dairy* by Lynley Dodd. The language is simple but effective, very descriptive, and also conveys a humorous and uniquely New Zealand story (where else do you find dairies?). As a dog-lover and dog-owner, I can also appreciate some of the escapades in which Hairy and his friends involve themselves. This poem has now become a must-read for New Zealand children and anything that encourages and inspires children to be read aloud to, and to read by themselves, is of great value. I have read this book to my own children many times and can still remember much of it by heart. I love all of Hairy Maclary's adventures but, as the original, this one would have to be my favourite.

Wendy Walker

Hairy Maclary from Donaldson's Dairy

Out of the gate and off for a walk
went Hairy Maclary from Donaldson's Dairy

and Hercules Morse as big as a horse
with Hairy Maclary from Donaldson's Dairy.

Bottomley Potts covered in spots,
Hercules Morse as big as a horse
and Hairy Maclary from Donaldson's Dairy,

Muffin McLay like a bundle of hay,
Bottomley Potts covered in spots,
Hercules Morse as big as a horse

and Hairy Maclary from Donaldson's Dairy.

Bitzer Maloney all skinny and bony,
Muffin McLay like a bundle of hay,
Bottomley Potts covered in spots,
Hercules Morse as big as a horse

and Hairy Maclary from Donaldson's Dairy.

Schnitzel von Krumm with a very low tum,
Bitzer Maloney all skinny and bony,
Muffin McLay like a bundle of hay,
Bottomley Potts covered in spots,
Hercules Morse as big as a horse

and Hairy Maclary from Donaldson's Dairy.

With tails in the air they trotted on down
past the shops and the park to the far end of town.
They sniffed at the smells and they snooped at each door,
when suddenly, out of the shadows
they saw . . .

SCARFACE CLAW
the toughest Tom in town.

'EEEEEOWWWFFTZ!'
said Scarface Claw.

Off with a yowl a wail and a howl,
a scatter of paws and a clatter of claws,
went Schnitzel von Krumm with a very low tum,
Bitzer Maloney all skinny and bony,
Muffin McLay like a bundle of hay,
Bottomley Potts covered in spots,
Hercules Morse as big as a horse
and Hairy Maclary from Donaldson's Dairy,

straight back home to bed.

LYNLEY DODD

Sir Tim Wallis

AVIATOR, FOUNDER OF WARBIRDS OVER WANAKA

Dear Lisa and Libby,

Thank you for your letter. Yes I would like to be involved and the poem I chose is 'If' by Rudyard Kipling, 1865–1936.

I chose this poem because of these four lines:

> If you can dream — and not make dreams your master,
> If you can think — and not make thoughts your aim;
> If you can meet with Triumph and Disaster
> And treat those two impostors just the same;

These are what I believe in.

Thank you both.

Sincerely,

Tim Wallis

If —

> If you can keep your head when all about you
>   Are losing theirs and blaming it on you;
> If you can trust yourself when all men doubt you
>   But make allowance for their doubting too;
> If you can wait and not be tired by waiting,
>   Or, being lied about, don't deal in lies,
> Or being hated, don't give way to hating,
>   And yet don't look too good, nor talk too wise:

If you can dream — and not make dreams your master,
    If you can think — and not make thoughts your aim;
If you can meet with Triumph and Disaster
    And treat those two impostors just the same;
If you can bear to hear the truth you've spoken
    Twisted by knaves to make a trap for fools,
Or watch the things you gave your life to, broken,
    And stoop and build 'em up with worn-out tools:

If you can make one heap of all your winnings
    And risk it on one turn of pitch-and-toss,
And lose, and start again at your beginnings
    And never breathe a word about your loss;
If you can force your heart and nerve and sinew
    To serve your turn long after they are gone,
And so hold on when there is nothing in you
    Except the Will which says to them: 'Hold on!;

If you can talk with crowds and keep your virtue,
    Or walk with kings — nor lose the common touch;
If neither foes nor loving friends can hurt you;
    If all men count with you, but none too much;
If you can fill the unforgiving minute
    With sixty seconds' worth of distance run,
Yours is the Earth and everything that's in it —
    And — which is more — you'll be a Man, my son!

RUDYARD KIPLING

Barbara Ward

SCULPTOR

Dear Libby,

Some things have the capacity, once absorbed, to never leave. For me, 'Randolph' is one of those things. It was written as a response to a sudden, senseless death of a much-loved friend. The words sit recessed like an ember that re-ignites into flame every time I hear them being carried along in their catafalque of mourning guitar and sombre drums. This wash of words and sound has ensured that this gentle soul remains forever captured in a time, never aging, like all lost friends, a kind of springboard for other memories to be brought back into focus. It rekindles the person, the time, the pain of the loss, the sheer left-behindness, all rolled into one. Randolph comes to visit then goes home. He's happy, I'm happy. Thanks Shayne.

Barbara Ward

Randolph's Going Home

The sergeant says he's just
back there so come with me
and somewhere Randolph's
gaily singing I'm set free
lonely, lonely like
a mother's cry

This anger seems the only
thing that never dies
and Venus lies alone
fanfares fade into drones
line up to cry cos Randolph's
going home

It's not that I'm big-headed
sending myself letters
it's just that no-one knows
myself better than me

While Venus lies alone
fanfares fade into drones
line up to cry
cos Randolph's going home

SHAYNE CARTER

Jennifer Ward-Lealand

ACTOR

Hi Libby and Esther,

I would be delighted to submit a poem for the *Dear to Me* anthology – and indeed the poem I have chosen leapt quickly to mind.

In 1981 I was touring small country towns with Murray Edmond's theatre company, The Town and Country Players. We travelled to some truly beautiful parts of the country but walking along the Waipawa River left a lasting impression.

During this tour I was preparing an audition for drama school – a speech from Chekhov's *The Seagull* – and was taking any opportunity to rehearse it, including on a walk along the river bed!

Not only is this a beautiful poem but it is also an honour to have had it dedicated to me.

Jennifer

Sentence on the Landscape
for Jennifer Ward-Lealand

Rehearsing Chekhov on the Waipawa River bed
she has trouble getting the line right.
Behind the willows where the drums of the

topdressing plane's engines beat, and
further back where wings of rain are breaking
on the Tararua snow, she is saying it

over and over – 'There is nothing for it,
there is nothing for it, we must go on
living, we must go on living, we shall

we shall we shall we shall go on living,
Uncle Vanya Uncle Vanya Uncle Vanya.'
There are graders grinding at the dump,

also behind the willows, there is a pillar
of dust rising, swallows dick and dive,
seagulls spin like boomerangs and magpies

float like ash out of the quenching green
wall of the pines. There is a correspondence
here being written out. The river clicks

its ten thousand tongues and the boulders
grumble and mutter under my feet.
Yet still she's there knocking out

the words, setting them up, knocking
them down, setting them up again, and
popping the trigger. And I heard the

moment when her voice turned and the
words drew up all the burden of their
correspondences, so when at night in the

black hum of the stage she speaks, she
will speak the speech of river, plane,
rain and snow, dust, ash, magpie, mountain,

swallow, seagull, willow, engine,
boulder, and her own throat will tell
these things like a river in her breath.

I bent down, in celebration, and
picked up a stone and threw it, and
followed it to where it landed and

bent and picked another up, and
threw again and the river bed was large
enough to go on doing this forever

MURRAY EDMOND

Cardinal Thomas Williams

ARCHBISHOP EMERITUS OF WELLINGTON

Dear Cleo and Libby,

'God's Grandeur' has ever been a favourite of mine, not so much because of its rhythms but because of its sustenance. During my 25 years as Archbishop of Wellington I lived on the edge of the city centre, looking out over acres of asphalt, concrete tower blocks and the teeming traffic. All the while my thoughts would go back to the Samoan villages where I had been parish priest. The poem, printed in the Breviary which Catholic clergy pray daily, was a sustaining influence. The realism of the first verse I readily recognised; the second never failed to put a new heart in me.

Yours sincerely,

Thomas Card. Williams

God's Grandeur

The world is charged with the grandeur of God.
    It will flame out, like shining from shook foil;
    It gathers to a greatness, like the ooze of oil
Crushed. Why do men then now not reck his rod?
Generations have trod, have trod, have trod;
    And all is seared with trade; bleared, smeared with toil;
    And wears man's smudge and shares man's smell: the soil
Is bare now, nor can foot feel, being shod.

And for all this, nature is never spent;
    There lives the dearest freshness deep down things;
And though the last lights off the black West went
    Oh, morning, at the brown brink eastward, springs –
Because the Holy Ghost over the bent
    World broods with warm breast and with ah! bright wings.

GERARD MANLEY HOPKINS

Dame Dorothy Winstone

EDUCATIONIST

Dear Esther,

One of the highlights of my teaching days at Seddon Memorial Technical College in Wellesley Street (now the home of the Auckland University of Technology), was a concert that the school put on in 1943 to raise money for the Patriotic Fund. My contribution was Choral Speaking. The girls in III Commercial C read together several poems and finally chose Hilaire Belloc's 'Tarantella', 'Vitai Lampada' by Sir Henry Newbolt, and A.A. Milne's 'The King's Breakfast'. A little childish you might think? Not a bit, it was sheer fun – the girls loved it, I loved it and the enthusiastic applause showed the audience loved it too. It was a thoroughly successful concert in every way.

With my best wishes for the success of your project,

Dame Dorothy Winstone

The King's Breakfast

The King asked
The Queen, and
The Queen asked
The Dairymaid:
'Could we have some butter for
The Royal slice of bread?'
The Queen asked the Dairymaid,
The Dairymaid
Said, 'Certainly,
I'll go and tell the cow

Now
Before she goes to bed.'

The Dairymaid
She curtsied,
And went and told the Alderney:
'Don't forget the butter for
The Royal slice of bread.'
The Alderney said sleepily:
'You'd better tell
His Majesty
That many people nowadays
Like marmalade
Instead.'

The Dairymaid
Said 'Fancy!'
And went to
Her Majesty.
She curtsied to the Queen, and
She turned a little red:
'Excuse me,
Your Majesty,
For taking of
The liberty,
But marmalade is tasty, if
It's very
Thickly
Spread.'

The Queen said
'Oh!'
And went to his Majesty:
'Talking of the butter for

The royal slice of bread,
Many people
Think that
Marmalade
Is nicer.
Would you like to try a little
Marmalade
Instead?'

The King said,
'Bother!'
And then he said,
'Oh deary me!'
The King sobbed, 'Oh deary me!'
And went back to bed.
'Nobody,'
He whimpered,
'Could call me
A fussy man;
I *only* want
A little bit
Of butter for
My bread!'

The Queen said,
'There, there!'
And went to
The Dairymaid.
The Dairymaid
Said, 'There, there!'
And went to the shed.
The cow said,
'There, there!
I didn't really

Mean it;
Here's milk for his porringer
And butter for his bread.'

The Queen took the butter
And brought it to
His Majesty.
The King said
'Butter, eh?'
And bounced out of bed.
'Nobody,' he said,
As he kissed her
Tenderly,
'Nobody, he said,
As he slid down
The banisters,
'Nobody,
My darling,
Could call me
A fussy man –
BUT
I do like a little bit of butter to my bread!'

A.A. MILNE

Gilbert Wong

COMMUNICATIONS MANAGER, HUMAN RIGHTS COMMISSION,
CONTRIBUTING WRITER, *METRO* MAGAZINE

Dear Lisa,

In the baby universe that is the long-settled New Zealand Chinese community Alison and I are related. She is the cousin of my cousins; our great-grandfathers came from southern China, dreaming of better lives for their children.

I chose this poem because it neatly ties up all that is good about family in seven lines and 50 words. When we were kids the kitchen was the centre of our universe and once you become a parent, you want the same for your children. The bowl of rice is the echo of China. I look at my daughter today, as she digs her mini-me chopsticks into her bowl for another mouthful of rice, and imagine her ancestors lined up watching over us, hoping we won't forget who they were.

Gilbert Wong

There's Always Things to Come
Back to the Kitchen for

a bowl of plain steamed rice
a piece of bitter dark chocolate
a slice of crisp peeled pear

a mother or father who understands
the kitchen is the centre of the universe

children who sail out on long elliptical orbits
and always come back, sometimes like comets,
    sometimes like moons

ALISON WONG

Acknowledgements

The publishers gratefully acknowledge the following authors, publishers, literary agencies and copyright holders for permission to reproduce the following poems:

'The Chiffonier' © Fleur Adcock, from *The Incident Book*, Oxford: Oxford University Press, 1986

'Refugee Blues' © estate of W.H. Auden, from *Collected Poems* by W.H. Auden, London: Faber and Faber, 2004

*'What Price Vietnam' © the Estate of Arapeta Awatere

'Horse is Dead' © Murray Ball. This letter and poem first appeared in the introduction to *Footrot Flats 7*, St Kilda West, Victoria: Orion Books, 1981–2

'Crossing Cook Strait', 'Song of the Years', 'High Country Weather', 'Farmhand', 'A Takapuna Businessman Considers His Son's Death in Korea', 'Lament for Barney Flanagan', 'A Pair of Sandals' and 'Ballad of Calvary Street' © the James K. Baxter Literary Trust, from *Collected Poems of James K. Baxter*, J.E. Weir (ed), Auckland: Oxford University Press, 2003

'Randolph's Going Home' © 1985 Shayne Carter and Peter Jefferies

'The Weeping Song' lyrics by Nick Cave. Reproduced with permission from Mushroom Music Publishing

'Elegy' © Jerry Chunn

'Boy' © Elizabeth Coleman

'The Skeleton of the Great Moa in the Canterbury Museum, Christchurch' and extract from 'Landfall in Unknown Seas' © Allen Curnow Literary Trust, from *Early Days Yet: New and Collected Poems 1941–1997*, Auckland: Auckland University Press, 1997

'I'm Nobody! Who are you?' by Emily Dickinson. Reprinted by permission of the publishers and Trustees of Amherst College from *The Poems of Emily Dickinson*, Thomas H. Johnson, ed., Cambridge, Mass.: The Belknap Press of Harvard University Press, Copyright © 1951, 1955, 1979, 1983 by the President and Fellows of Harvard College

'Hairy Maclary from Donaldson's Dairy' © Lynley Dodd and Mallinson Rendel, originally published as a children's picture book, *Hairy Maclary from Donaldson's Dairy* by Lynley Dodd, Wellington: Mallinson Rendel, 1983

'Liverpool' © Michael Donaghy, from *Dances Learned Late Last Night: Poems 1975–1995*, London: Macmillan, 2000

'The Search' © Rita Dove, from *Mother Love*, New York: W.W. Norton, 1995

'At Grass Street' © Frances Edmond and the Estate of Lauris Edmond, from *Scenes from a Small City*, Wellington: Daphne Brasell Associates, 1994

'Sentence on the Landscape' © Murray Edmond, from *Letters and Paragraphs: Poems*, Christchurch: Caxton, 1987

*'The Journey of the Magi' © the Estate of T.S. Eliot, from *T.S. Eliot Collected Poems 1909–1962*, London: Faber and Faber, 1963

'Uncertainties' © the Estate of D.J.

Enright, from *The Terrible Shears: Scenes from a Twenties Childhood*, London: Chatto & Windus, 1973

'Not Understood' © the A.R.D. Fairburn Literary Estate, from *Collected Poems*, Christchurch: Pegasus, 1966

'The Lament of the Nun of Beare', version © Fiona Farrell

'Dunedin Poem' by Janet Frame © the Janet Frame Literary Trust, reprinted with permission from *The Pocket Mirror* (first published in 1967) in *Janet Frame, Stories and Poems*, Auckland: Vintage, 2004

'Home Thoughts' © the Denis Glover Estate and Pia Glover, from *An Anthology of New Zealand Poetry in English*, by Jenny Bornholdt, Gregory O'Brien and Mark Williams eds., Oxford: Oxford University Press, 1998

'The Tollund Man' © Seamus Heaney, from *Selected Poems 1965-1975* by Seamus Heaney, London: Faber and Faber, 1980

'Beware the Man' and 'My Father Today' © Sam Hunt, from *Sam Hunt Selected Poems*, Auckland: Penguin, 1987

Extract from 'The Beaches' by Robin Hyde © Derek Challis, from *Houses by the Sea and the Later Poems of Robin Hyde*, edited by Gloria Rawlinson, Christchurch: Caxton, 1952

'The Literary Man Tends a Modern Garden' © Kevin Ireland, from *Literary Cartoons*, Auckland: Islands/Hurricane, 1977; and 'Stones as Sculptor' © Kevin Ireland, from *Islands*, Christchurch: March 1980

'Secular Litany' © Mrs M.J. Joseph, from *Imaginary Islands: Poems* by M.K. Joseph, Auckland: Whitcombe and Tombs, 1950

'Glimpses of Ecstasy over the Pacific' © Kapka Kassabova. This is an earlier version of 'Middle-aged Couple Watch a Pacific Sunset', from *Geography for the Lost* by Kapka Kassabova, Auckland: Auckland University Press/Tarset, Northumberland: Bloodaxe, 2007

'Sleeping Arrangements' © Richard Langston, from *Henry, Come See the Blue*, Wellington: Fitzbeck Publishing, 2005

'At Grass' © Philip Larkin and The Marvell Press, reprinted from *The Less Deceived: Poems* by permission of The Marvell Press, England and Australia

'For the Union Dead', Robert Lowell, from *Life Studies and For the Union Dead* by Robert Lowell, New York: Noonday Press (a division of Farrar, Straus & Giroux, Inc.), 1967

'Timepiece' © Cilla McQueen, from *Homing In*, Dunedin: McIndoe, 1984; 'Luncheon Cove' © Cilla McQueen and University of Otago Press, from *Markings*, Dunedin: University of Otago Press, 2000

'Children' © Bill Manhire, from *Collected Poems*, Wellington: Victoria University Press, 1982

'Cargoes' © The Society of Authors as Literary Representative of the Estate of John Masefield, from *Ballads and Poems*, London: Elkin Mathews, 1910; 'Sea-Fever' © The Society of Authors as Literary Representative of the Estate of John Masefield, from *Salt-Water Ballads*, London: Grant Richards, 1902

'On the Swag' © R.A.K. Mason Literary Estate, Hocken Library, Dunedin, reprinted with permission

'Child at Heart' © Bernice Mene

'Bump!' and 'Carrington Briggs' © Spike Milligan Productions Limited

'The Storm' © Moana Mourie

'For Everyone', a translation of
'Para todos' by Pablo Neruda, from
Fully Empowered: Plenos poderes,
translated by Alistair Reid, New York:
Farrar, Straus & Giroux, 2001; 'If You
Forget Me' by Pablo Neruda, from
The Captain's Verses, New York: New
Directions, 2004

'The Day Lady Died' © the Estate of
Frank O'Hara, from *Selected Poems*,
Manchester: Carcanet Press Limited,
1991

'Don't Knock the Rawleigh's Man' ©
Vincent O'Sullivan, from *The Rose
Ballroom and Other Poems*, Dunedin:
McIndoe, 1982

Kia Whakapākeha Au I Ahau
© Merimeri Penfold

'The Dark Side of Trees' © Cecil
Rajendra, from *Hour of the Assassins
& Other Poems*, London: Bogle-
L'Ouverture Publications, 1983

Last Evenings on Earth © John Reynolds
2006; photograph by Patrick Reynolds
photography

'The Cutting' © Sam Sampson,
from *Rolling Thunder: The Spirit of
Karekare* by Bob Harvey, Auckland:
Exisle Press, 2001

'The St Columbo's Cat' © Che'den
Strickson-Pua and Jane Filemu, from
Matua by Rev. Mua Strickson-Pua,
Auckland: Pohutukawa Press, 2006

'Cows' © The Topp Twins

'After' © Brian Turner, from *All That
Blue Can Be*, Dunedin: McIndoe, 1989;
'Cricket' © Brian Turner, from *Taking
Off*, Wellington: Victoria University
Press, 2001

'Hotere' © Hone Tuwhare, from
Come Rain, Hail: Poems, Dunedin:

Bibliography Room, University of
Otago, 1970; 'No Ordinary Sun' ©
Hone Tuwhare, from *No Ordinary
Sun*, Auckland: Blackwood and Janet
Paul, 1964; 'Papa-tu-a-nuku' © Hone
Tuwhare, from *Making a Fist of it*,
Dunedin: Jackstraw Press, 1978

'Parents & Children' © Albert Wendt,
from *Shaman of Visions*, Auckland:
Auckland University Press, 1984

'There's Always Things to Come Back
to the Kitchen for' © Alison Wong, from
Cup, Wellington: Steele Roberts, 2006

'Flex' © Dave Yetton, from *The Jean
Paul Sartre Experience*, Flying Nun,
1987

'He Will Come Back, the One I'm
Waiting for' © Ahmed Zaoui (interpreted
by Riemke Ensing), from *Migrant Birds:
24 Contemplations*, Nelson: Craig
Potton Publishing, 2005

Index of Titles and First Lines

Index of Poets